To Make That Future—Now!

A History of the Manchester and Salford Trades Council

The coming hope, the future day,
When wrong to right shall bow,
And but a little courage, man!
To make that future Now!

The song of the future

ERNEST JONES

by

EDMUND and RUTH FROW

1976
E. J. MORTEN (PUBLISHERS)
DIDSBURY MANCHESTER
ENGLAND

First published 1976. E. J. Morten, Warburton St., Didsbury, Manchester, England
© Edmund and Ruth Frow, 1976.

I S B N
CLOTH—   0 85972 025 0
PAPER—   0 85972 026 8

T

Printed in Great Britain by
The Scolar Press Limited, Ilkley, Yorkshire

1002290124

"The coming hope, the future day,

When wrong to right shall bow,

And but a little courage, man!

To make that future - NOW."

> The Song of the Future,
> Ernest Jones.

TO MAKE THAT FUTURE - NOW!

A History of the Manchester and Salford
Trades Council

by

Edmund and Ruth Frow

CONTENTS

ILLUSTRATIONS

Opposite Page

Acknowledgements

The authors would like to express their gratitude to all who have helped them in compiling this history.

The following organisations have made records and reports available:

Amalgamated Union of Engineering Workers, Manchester District Committee.

Lancashire Box, Packing Case and General Woodworkers Society.

Manchester Central Library.

National Graphical Association, Manchester Branch.

Union of Shop, Distributive and Allied Workers, General Office.

University of Manchester Arts Library.

Working Class Movement Library, Manchester.

Of the many individuals who have read the manuscript and loaned material, the list that follows is representative only:

Allan Clinton, Francis Dean, Fred Flood, Sol Gadian, Arthur Harvey, Harry Ingle, Mick Jenkins, Dennis Maher, the late John Mahon, Mrs. Newbold.

Foreword

Manchester has had a long history of struggle to build the present labour movement but this story of the development of the Trades Council is short. There are two good reasons for this brevity.

During the air-raids on the City in 1940, the Offices of the Council were blitzed and most of the records were destroyed. This has meant that the authors have had to rely on press reports and such material as has been preserved by unions and individuals. That is why it would appear that much of the Council work has been spectacular and colourful in terms of demonstrations and meetings. Only these events are reported in the press. The daily routine of trade union affairs which the Trades Council has persistently pursued for over a hundred years is not publicised. It is not the material of which the more newsworthy events are built. This history has therefore been written from the point of view of the peaks of interest and activity and the hard grind that has made these possible is, perhaps, obscured.

The second reason why there is not a more weighty tome to honour the century of struggle in which the Trades Council has consistently played a leading part is the wish of the authors that this history should be available to the present and future workers who are engaged in efforts to raise their standards of living. These workers need and deserve their history in a format and at a price to fit their pocket. If it is read and discussed in factories, in offices, shops and schools and strength for the future gained from studying the past, then this short history of the Manchester and Salford Trades Council will have played its part in building that future - now!

Francis Dean

Chapter 1

Manchester and its Working Class. Early Attempts at Organisation.

> "Manchester is the seat of the
> most powerful Unions, the central
> point of Chartism, the place which
> numbers most Socialists. The
> more the factory system has taken
> possession of a branch of industry,
> the more the working men employed
> in it participate in the labour
> movement." [1]

Manchester earned its title of
Cottonopolis early in the nineteenth century.
The rapidly developing cotton industry which
relied, at first, on the swift streams of the
hilly country, soon moved, with the advent of
steam, to factory towns. The growth of the
cotton industry necessitated the building of
factories and houses. It led to the development
of transport and fostered the engineering
industry. By the middle of the century
Manchester had become the pattern of a
thriving industrial town with its centre devoted
to commerce, its heavily populated working
class districts encircling the warehouses and
offices and the outer ring of better houses
bordering on the country beyond.

Although the growth of Manchester's
population followed an upward curve throughout
this early period rising by about fifty percent
in each ten year census, the prosperity of the

town did not follow the same smooth path.
Karl Marx noted, "The life of modern industry
becomes a series of periods of moderate
activity, prosperity, over-production, crisis
and stagnation. The uncertainty and instability
to which machinery subjects the employment,
and consequently the conditions of existence, of
the operatives, become normal, owing to these
periodic changes of the industrial cycle."[2]
An acute observer of the Manchester scene
wrote, "first the merchants were affected by
the stagnation of trade, and they again
influenced the manufacturers, by no longer
requiring their wares. Thus factory after
factory was stopped, and its owners became
bankrupts. This stopping of the factories
turned numbers of labourers out of employment.
All the smaller trades people and shopkeepers
now suffered from the failure of their custom;
and the masons, carpenters and bricklayers
could get no work, because no new houses were
built and those already building were stopped.
Next, the butchers, bakers and grocers began
to go down in the world, on account of the
decrease of their custom, and they again
affected the farmers and gardeners in the
neighbourhood of the towns."[3]
    Spells of industrial activity in which all
shared in the boom of overtime working
alternated with periods of unemployment when
craftsmen and labourers alike joined the queues
of those who, "desperately continue to hope and
try, and day after day walk long distances, and
wait patiently for hours outside workshop gates,
in vain search for the work they cannot find."[4]
At times of slump, the working people of

2

Manchester, herded in slums in Ancoats, Ardwick, and the townships surrounding the commercial centre, pawned their dearest possessions to provide food. These were times "to make a brave man eat his heart out, and cause the most cheerful to despond... when men not only suffer the woes of want themselves, but are maddened by their sense of powerlessness to save their wives and children from those woes."[5]

Even in better times, the lot of the worker was never far from unhappiness. He lived in "a dense urban area whose noxious defects provided spectacular material for the pioneer public health movement."[6] Descriptions of the Manchester slums have provided material for a number of official reports as well as background for novels. By the 1851 Exhibition, there were over a thousand different manufacturing trades in the town. They were mainly cotton mills, engineering works, saw mills and rubber works, with also a number of miscellaneous works such as box-making, umbrella making, confectionary, garment making, and furniture manufacture. The workers lived among the mills, factories, yards and warehouses in "dreary little streets ... mainly of the 'two up and two down' type ... The actual density of houses - apart from commercial buildings - is about 44.8 to the acre. There are no gardens or trees - nothing to relieve the deadly monotony and greyness of its mean streets - except perhaps the massive shapes of its gaunt factories and the canals ... black and strewn with rubbish."[7]

At work, in the factories the workers were

subjected to "dust, dirt, stunning noises, unpleasant smells and close air."[8] One commentator describing Orell's Mill said, "This factory is one of the best built of any; yet I found the air intolerably close and suffocating in some parts. I was also sorry to observe the terrible narrowness of the passes between dangerous machines and their restless and gigantic arms and wheels; in these passes the floor was also extremely smooth and slippery."[9] Work began at six and continued until eight at night, with half hour breaks at eight and four and an hour between twelve and one. In such conditions it is not surprising that the Manchester Hospital dealt with the highest rate of accidents of any in Europe. Upwards of four thousand serious accidents were treated there every year. In 1843 it was noted, "The statistical tables of the hospital show that one in every eighty-seven of the inhabitants is seriously injured or wounded every year. Or if an average duration of thirty-five years be allowed for the life of every inhabitant, two serious wounds are suffered during life by every five inhabitants."[10]

Many problems of our day had their roots in those early factory processes. It was noted in a book about Manchester boys written at the beginning of this century, "the more monotonous the machine work, and the less it calls for intelligence on the part of those engaged in it, the more unruly do such lads become in their spare hours. The entire want of a mental occupation during the day, or of any early training giving the slightest zest for such occupation during leisure hours, often causes lads employed at this kind of labour to become very unruly at night and to acquire many undesirable habits."[11]

The fact that today there are fewer boys and girls undertaking education beyond the statutory age in the North West than in most other areas of the country probably springs from the tradition of child labour which blotted the copybook of the industrial scene from the early days of the infants in the cotton mills sweeping under the vast moving jennies until it was finally ended in the Fisher Education Act of 1918. There are some alive today who began work as a Half-timer at the age of twelve, spending half their time in school and the other half at work. George Tomlinson, the Minister of Education who steered the 1944 Education Act through Parliament wrote of his own experiences. "As I look back upon it I think of the days when I attempted to find my way to work on the arm of my father, finishing my sleep as I went through the fields which divided the factory from the home in which we lived, and I wonder how people could manufacture such phrases as 'beneficial employment'. Beneficial to whom? There was only one reason why I went into the mill at twelve years of age. Make no mistake about it. I know the reason. It meant 2s. 3d. per week in the home, in which at that time there were seven people with an average wage coming in of 26s. per week. The 2s. 3d. per week made it easier for my mother to come somewhat nearer to balancing the family budget. That was the only beneficial aspect of that employment to which I was sent. My fingers were nimble at twelve, and my father's were nimble at eight."[12]

5

Over the years there has never been a lack of issues confronting the working class in Manchester. Their hours of work, the conditions in their factories, the savage exploitation of women and children, the slums in which they lived, have all, from time to time, figured in the campaigns of the trade union movement to secure a more dignified way of life for the workers. The Manchester and Salford Trades Council has, over the years, taken the leadership and developed propaganda and activity which has made the life of a worker in mid-twentieth century Manchester very different from that of his ancestors a hundred years earlier.

Early Attempts at Organisation

As the changing Manchester scene became more industrial and more densely populated, so sharp polarisation into those who worked for their wages, the workers, and those who owned the factories and machines, the masters, developed. Before 1824 and the repeal of the Combination Acts, which made trade unions illegal, there were a number of sharp clashes. The effect of trade cycles on the lives of workers who were barely at subsistence level at the best of times, made desperate action inevitable. Frustration at lack of communication and isolation from the seat of power due to the unrepresentative character of the House of Commons gave rise to the movement for Reform of Parliament and the traumatic experience of the Peterloo Massacre. Mass action, calling for a high degree of organisation, naturally taught workers much about the value of combination. It also developed thinkers, poets and leaders such as Benjamin

Stott, James Leach and John Doherty. Such men recognised that trade union activity was essential for the achievement of social and political aims. Before the formation of the Trades Council there was a strong tradition of joint action by Trades' Societies to combine on specific issues. As early as 1818, the cotton spinners, the first new skilled trade created by the industrial revolution, made an effort to induce other trades in the Manchester District to join together in a Philanthropic Society. It was successful, but short lived.

The first attempt to combine under the name of 'Trades Council' was made in 1837, when a meeting of the "United Trades Council of Manchester and Salford" was held in the Corn Exchange. The meeting was part of a campaign conducted by the trade union movement to rally support for the Glasgow Cotton Spinners. The subject of the Manchester meeting was "Whig Tyranny and The Glasgow Cotton Spinners". It was significant that the attack on the Glasgow spinners was recognised as a political move and likely to spread if allowed to succeed. The thousand people at the meeting heard J. R. Richardson, Christopher Dean, Edward Curren and Joseph Raynor Stephens, all of whom played a part in the Chartist movement as it developed in the succeeding years.

The following year, on Monday 25th September, 1838, a huge crowd estimated at three hundred thousand assembled on Kersal Moor to adopt the six points of the Charter. Even heavy rain could not disperse the people who reacted strongly to the mention by Hodgetts, who moved the resolution to adopt the Charter, of the events of Peterloo. Banners which had been carried in August 1819 were brought out again on that day nearly twenty years later. There were also banners from trades' contingents. These included the Tailors, Smiths and Wheelwrights, Dyers, Joiners, Fustian Shearers, Callenderers, Painters, Men's Boot and Shoe Makers, Marble Masons, Masons, Ladies' Shoe Makers, Labourers, Bricklayers, Marble Polishers, Sawyers, Spinners and Farriers. There were also representatives from the metal trades, the Mechanics, Smiths, Moulders, Engineers and Millwrights. These trades already called themselves the "United Trades" and met in a loose federation.

When a General Strike broke out in 1842, the two distinct sections that gave rise to leadership were the trades represented by the power loom weavers and the metal workers, such as the mechanics. Although the strike began in Stalybridge as the result of a wages cut in the cotton mills, it rapidly spread and Manchester became the storm centre. The mechanics organised a Conference in the Carpenters Hall on 11th and 12th of August where a resolution was carried to change the character of the strike and to remain out until the demands outlined in the People's Charter were conceded. The immediate implementation of the Charter was not achieved, but the lessons of solidarity in action were not lost.

The engineers' strike of 1852 and the fustian dyers' in July 1853 both reinforced the need for solidarity. Sixteen-thousand fustian dyers were employed in and around Manchester. They asked for an extra sixpence an hour. When it was refused, they began a strike which continued for seventeen weeks. Meanwhile, their employers trained twelve-thousand other operatives to take their place and they were defeated. This gave rise to such hardship that in March 1854, "The Trades Defence Association of Manchester" was formed. This was a committee of operatives in a variety of local trades, pledged to give mutual support in future strikes, and it represented a serious attempt on the part of Manchester trades' unions to join under one organisation for defence and protection. A similar association was organised nationally, but functioned in Manchester. This was the "Labour Parliament". The basic aim was support for Preston cotton operatives who were on strike. Ernest Jones, the Chartist, campaigned for a "National Labour Revenue" of a penny a week levy on wages to provide a defence fund. Although this Parliament was supported by such redoubtable leaders as E. Clark Cropper of the Amalgamated Association of Miners and a Chartist and John Teer, a poet who was Secretary of the Manchester Fine Spinners Association, it failed to develop the mass movement that Ernest Jones had hoped to see.

The Manchester industrial scene changed dramatically over the years that immediately followed the Chartist movement. 1851, the year of the Great Exhibition, was possibly the apex of development without competition. Britain remained the "workshop of the world" for a number of years, but international competition soon caught up and eventually passed British industrial output. While the list of trades in Manchester at the beginning of the century had represented mainly domestic workers who worked in their own home, or cotton trade workers in factories, by 1861, when the London

Trades' Council issued a national Trades' Union Directory, the scene was vastly different. There were then ninety-seven Trades' Societies listed in the Manchester section. Among them were ten Branches of the Amalgamated Society of Engineers, The Carpenters and Joiners, the Boot and Shoe Makers, the Hydraulic Packers, the Hookers and the Bricklayers Labourers. Each had three Branches, while the Coachbuilders, Boilermakers, Managers and Overlookers and the Makers-up, had one Branch each.

During the sixties, the threads of working class activity coalesced. Political consciousness developed around agitation for a widening of the franchise. Awareness of the benefits of mutual assistance grew through the work of the Trades' Defence Association. Polarisation into 'The Two Nations' stressed the desirability of class based combinations, and both workers and employers formed associations. The stage was set for a more permanent organisation to unite the Manchester trades.

References

[1] Frederick Engels, The Condition of the Working Class in England, Panther edition, 1969, p. 266

[2] Karl Marx, Capital, Volume I, Moscow, 1959, p. 453

[3] J. G. Kohl, England and Wales, 1844, p. 115

[4] (Thomas Wright) The Journeyman Engineer, The Great Unwashed (1868) Kelly reprint 1970, p. 286

[5] ibid., pp286/7

[6] Manchester and District Regional Survey Society, Housing Needs of Ancoats in Relation to the Greenwood Act, Manchester, 1930, p. 3 (pamphlet)

[7] ibid., p. 8

[8] J. G. Kohl, op. cit., p. 126

[9] ibid., p. 122

[10] ibid., p. 108

[11] Charles E. B. Russell, Manchester Boys, Manchester, 1905, p. 13.

[12] Fred Blackburn, George Tomlinson, A Biography, 1954, p. 12.

Chapter 2

The Formation of the Trades Council

"Trades Unions ask not for grace;
they simply seek justice. Their
political value is so great, and is
also increasing, and should they
be longer denied justice, they may
be prepared to sink their several
political creeds, and unite together
with their strength and influence to
throw their weight into that scale
which shall elect to represent their
interests and promote their aims."

Trades Unions Defended
    by William Henry Wood (1870).

Arising out of activity around the agitation
for legislative reform, a conference of trades
was held in Sheffield in July 1866. One of the
aims of this conference was to secure the
establishment of Courts of Conciliation and
Arbitration. Among the hundred and thirty
delegates were W. H. Wood and S. C. Nicholson
of the Manchester Typographical Society. On
their return from Sheffield, they issued
invitations to a group of trade unionists to form
a provisional committee with a view to starting
an "Association of Organised Trades" in
Manchester. The Committee met every
Thursday at The Three Crowns in King Street,
Salford.

Manchester trade unionists were prominent
in the agitation for the extension of the franchise.
They supported the Reform League, which called

12

for manhood suffrage and a ballot vote. When the League called a demonstration on Monday afternoon, 24th September, 1866, the workers insisted that all factories be closed for the afternoon. The demonstration was held on Campfields, which was known as Knott Mill Fairground, and, in spite of the pouring rain, twenty-thousand people listened to the speakers. Among the contingents that carried banners in the march were the Hulme and Chorlton Carpenters and Joiners, the Ancoats Glass Blowers, the Bakers' Society and the Operative Stonemasons.

It was in this atmosphere that the Provisional Committee called an inaugural meeting of the Manchester and Salford Trades Council on 9th October, 1866. This meeting was adjourned until 9th November when S. C. Nicholson was elected as the first President and W. H. Wood the Secretary. John Pike, the landlord of The Three Crowns and a file cutter by trade, was elected as Treasurer. He allowed the Council to use the large room in his pub. The Council delegates elected ten representatives which, together with the Officers, comprised the Executive Committee.

The Council represented mainly the skilled trades and only men. Many of them were organised in small local craft unions. The ten Council members were Timbs, Bookbinder; Shorrocks, Tailor; Cooper, Plasterer; Atkin, General Union of Joiners; Ridge, Ironfounders; Lawther, House Painter; Parson, Lithographer; Fairbrother, Baker; Figgins, Sadler; and Schofield, Mule Spinner. The Engineers and Fine Spinners did not immediately join the Council, and the final adoption of the Rules was

13

left until these two important Societies cooperated.

W. H. Wood and S. C. Nicholson were Conservative working men, but other active members of the Council were Radicals. These included Peter Shorrocks of the Tailors, Malcolm MacLeod, an Engineer, William MacDonald of the Operative Housepainters and R. H. Slatter of the Typographical Society. The political division on the Council led many times to individual unions taking part in activity when the Council itself was unable to do so. A demonstration organised jointly by the Reform League and the middle class Reform Union was supported by a conference at which William Macdonald took the Chair. It was held in May, 1867, and over forty trade union branches were represented. These included eight from the Amalgamated Society of Engineers, five from the Amalgamated Society of Carpenters and Joiners, and five from the General Union of Carpenters. The conference decided to take part in the demonstration and they marched from Stevenson's Square carrying the banners of the Ironmoulders, Boilermakers Machine Workers, Amalgamated Engineers, Rollermakers, Ironpressers, Planers, Grinders, Whitesmiths, Brass Finishers, Masons, Painters, Plasterers, Carpenters, Joiners, Cabinet Makers, Tailors, Coopers, Corkcutters, Sadlers, Bleachers, Cotton Spinners, Glass Cutters, Glass Blowers, Boot and Shoe Makers, Bookbinders and Bakers. Twenty-five bands grouped around the six platforms in Hullard Park and there were "union banners and flags beyond precedent."[1] Among the speakers were Ernest Jones, the Chartist and Elijah Dixon.

When the Council took a decision to avoid identification with any political movement, the Radicals formed "The Trade Unionists' Political Association" to press for the extension of the franchise. William MacDonald was President and Malcolm MacLeod Secretary. Although mounting agitation compelled the Government to extend the vote to the lower middle class and higher paid workers, when the 1868 Election was held on the new electoral roll no working class candidate was returned.

Trade union action to prevent the implementation of legislation intended to curb or restrict the power of the organised workers was not the first. Soon after its formation, the Manchester and Salford Trades Council became involved in discussions on the status of trade unions in relation to the law. Although trades unions had achieved legality with the repeal of the Combination Acts in 1824, they could still be prosecuted under common law for conspiracy.

The London Working Men's Association called a conference in St. Martin's Hall, London from March 5th to 8th, 1867, to "discuss the status of trade societies" and "to devise the most effective means by which trade societies may obtain the protection of the law for their funds." [2] W. H. Wood, who represented Manchester Trades Council, played a prominent part in these proceedings. He was elected to the Conference General Purposes Committee and also to a special committee formed to place evidence before the Royal Commission on Trade Unions. The conference adopted a Bill of Trade Union Rights and Wood moved a successful resolution calling on the Trades Unions to convene public meetings and from them to send petitions to the Government along the lines outlined in the Bill.

In February, 1868, the Trades Unionists' Political Association sent a deputation to see Thomas Bazely and Jacob Bright, the Manchester Members of Parliament. The Trades Council was represented by S. C. Nicholson who raised the question of the state of the law relating to trades unions. Although the Molestation of Workmen Act of 1859 had, in theory, made picketing legal, unions were constantly attacked in the Courts for being 'in restraint of trade' and for conspiracy. During the discussion, MacLeod and MacDonald pursued these questions with the M. P. s and obtained satisfactory assurances of their support.

In June, 1869, the Council launched a campaign to win support for the Trade Union Bill put forward by two sympathetic M. P. s, Thomas Hughes and A. J. Mundella. S. C. Nicholson presided at a trade union demonstration on Knott Mill Fairground where W. H. Wood was the main speaker. In 1871, the Home Secretary introduced the Trade Union Act in Parliament. This was carried and laid down that no member of a trade union could be prosecuted for being "in restraint of trade". The Act also gave protection to Union funds. However, a second Act, "The Criminal Law Amendment Act" in the same year, made the law on picketting and coercion more oppressive. In the same year that it was enacted, seven women were sent to prison for saying "BAH" to a blackleg.

Naturally, the Council gave full support to the first Act but opposed the second. In June, 1872, a demonstration was organised to demand the repeal of the "Criminal Law Amendment Act". A call for a nine hour day was also made. Thirty-five trades were represented and they marched in a mile long procession with thirty bands. The following year a similar demonstration was again held in June and the Council debated both the "Criminal Law Amendment Act" and the pernicious "Master and Servant Act". A workman who wilfully broke his contract, either by absenting himself from work or by leaving his job, could be tried on a criminal charge and was liable for three months imprisonment. The master, on the other hand, could only be summoned for payment of wages due to the worker. There were other aspects of the Act which were blatantly weighted in the master's favour and which were flagrently unjust towards the workman.

Following similar action on a national scale, the Government set up a Royal Commission on Trade Unions. This was a favourite device for avoiding the necessity for action. The inevitable delay aroused sharp criticism from the trade unions. It was not until 1875 that R.A. Cross, the Home Secretary, introduced legislation into the House of Commons. A keen debate took place in the Trades Council and a resolution supporting the Government Bill was amended to demand the repeal of certain objectionable clauses. The Bill was largely amended in Committee to the satisfaction of the Council and the "Conspiracy and Protection of Property Act, 1875" replaced the "Criminal Law Amendment

17

Act". The legal obstacles to picketting were not removed by the new Act and persecution and prosecution of trade unionists continued.

From its earliest days, the Council gave support to trades in dispute. This support was not reserved for local unions and in 1868, the London Tailors were assisted. 1874 was a year of fraternal solidarity. Nottingham Bleachers were supported in their dispute and in June, the Council organised a massive demonstration to rally sympathetic action for the Agricultural Labourers.

The organisation of the depressed and downtrodden land workers had been initiated by Joseph Arch in February, 1872, when he addressed a historic meeting beneath the village Chestnut Tree at Wellesbourne. By May, 1873, the Union had nearly seventy-two thousand members organised in over nine-hundred branches. Wages, in some districts, were as low as seven shillings for a working week of six, twelve-hour days. Attempts in 1874 to establish a basic minimum of sixteen shillings a week led to a lockout. A Relief Committee was set up to mobilise support for the destitute men and their families and the Council gave full support. It was decided to organise a demonstration in Manchester on 20th June, 1874. Trade Unionists from many places in Lancashire and Yorkshire rallied to the City and were drawn up four abreast to the number of some twenty thousand. The trades succeeded each other in alphabetical order, each with its banner and trade emblem. The many bands played appropriate tunes such as "The Farmer's Boy" and "The Fine Old

THE BISHOP OF MANCHESTER

ON THE

LOCK-OUT OF THE AGRICULTURAL LABOURERS.

To the Editor of the "Times."

SIR,—May I ask for your insertion of a few lines—not about the Bengal Famine, with which my name has been associated far more prominently than I desired, but upon a subject of hardly secondary importance, and which may even bring the fact of famine, or at least of dearth, much closer to our doors than some of us, perhaps, are dreaming of as possible ?

Are the farmers of England going mad ? Are they about to add to another exemplification to the old adage, " *Quos Deus vult perdere, prius dementat !*[*] What can they possibly imagine will be the issue of this suicidal lock-out, which has already thrown 4000 labourers on the fund of the Agricultural Union, and which seems to be spreading like a pestilence in the Eastern Counties ? Can they, as reasonable men, able to read the signs of the times, suppose that this measure will stave off for any appreciable time the solution of the inevitable question—What is the equitable wage to pay the men who till their ground, tend their stock, gather in their harvest ? If a lock-out could be at any time regarded as a rational mode of attempting to evade this difficulty, what a moment have the farmers of the Eastern Counties chosen for it ! With much of their Spring corn still unsown, with all their root-crops needing to be prepared, and all their harvests to come, no wise man would counsel them that this is the time to agitate the labour market with a disturbance of its equilibrium. And what can they hope to gain by this ill-advised procedure ? They may drive their best labourers either to the other side of the Atlantic, or into some new field of employment ; they may fill the workhouses with able-bodied men and women, stripped of their homes and all that has made life, amid their many hardships, still dear to them. But will they have settled the wage question ? Will they have improved their own condition or prospects ? *Will they have conquered ?* From the increased facilities of communication, agricultural labourers in the South and East of England know that their fellows in the North are receiving 18s. or £1 a week ; they will ask themselves the question, why they should be receiving 20 or 30 per cent less ?

Everyone must have noticed that the language of the leaders of the movement, at first studiously moderate, has become more violent, and in some cases even insurrectionary and menacing. The most frightful thing that could happen for English society would be a " peasants' war." Yet that is what we are driving to, if insane counsels of mutual exasperation prevail.

But it is not to motives of fear, but to the higher motives of equity and reason, that I would appeal. Are the demands—even the highest demands—of the agricultural labourers, when all the surroundings of the situation are considered, really unreasonable and inordinate ? Can a man, at the present prices of the necessaries of life, maintain himself and his family, I will not say in comfort, but even with a sufficiency of food, fuel, and clothing to enable him to put his full strength into his work, on a smaller income than 15s. or 16s. a week ? And if farmers say they cannot afford to pay this rate of wages with their present rentals, *and can prove the truth of this statement,* then rents must come down—an unpleasant thing even to contemplate for those who will spend the rent of a 300-acre farm on a single ball or upon a pair of high-stepping carriage horses, but nevertheless one of the things inevitable.

I am no lover of the principles of Trade-Unionism, but they have been forced upon the working classes by the inequitable use of the power of capital.

I hope it is not too late to tell the farmers that in locking out their labourers they are making a terrible mistake, and that its sure result, even if apparently successful, will be to precipitate the day when they who lived directly by the cultivation of the soil will be divided into two hostile armies, and those feelings of mutual confidence and a combined interest which once made life in a country village so much happier a thing than life in a manufacturing town will be for ever destroyed. I appeal to the intelligence, and even to the self-interest, of a body of men who certainly have as much good sense and kindly feeling as any other class among their countrymen to avert this dire catastrophe.

I remain, Sir,

Your obedient Servant,

J. MANCHESTER.

Manchester, March 31.

* " Those whom the gods intend to destroy they first drive mad."

PRINTED IN THE GREAT TRADES PROCESSION AT MANCHESTER, ON SATURDAY, JUNE 20TH, 1874, IN BEHALF OF THE LOCKED-OUT AGRICULTURAL LABOURERS.

THE LATE TRADES' UNION DEMONSTRATION AT MANCHESTER IN FAVOUR OF THE LABOURERS

English Gentlemen". The Manchester
Typographical Society had a dray on which was
mounted a printing press. As it proceeded
along the route, a letter, written by the Bishop
of Manchester[3] and published in the "Times",
calling for justice for the agricultural workers,
was printed and sold to raise funds.
Words of songs to be sung along the route
were issued. They were called 'Songs of the
Labourers' and one sung to Rule Britannia
began,
" When Britain's serfs, at
                heaven's command,
    Arose and broke from
                slavery's chain,
    This was the charter of the land,
    And guardian angels sung the strain,
        Rule Britannia,
                Britannia rules the knaves,
        Britons never shall be slaves".

The grand march started at four o'clock
from Albert Square and proceeded along Peter
Street, Oxford Street, Piccadilly, Market
Street, Blackfriars, Chapel Street and New
Bailey Street to Pomona Gardens.[4]   Fifty-
thousand people greeted the marchers as they
entered the Gardens and the speakers who were
due to begin at six o'clock had to postpone the
meeting until eight, to allow the crowds to
assemble. There were six platforms. W. H.
Wood took the Chair on one and Peter
Shorrocks on another. Joseph Arch also
addressed the huge gathering which donated
the collection to the Relief Fund.

In 1877 trade was bad and the cotton
employers reduced wages. Eighteen hundred

spinners in Bolton went on strike in protest and ten thousand other workers became involved. In November, the employers enforced a five per cent wage reduction and four months later, in March, 1878, a further ten per cent. By April, the Trades Council found itself involved in helping to organise support for the ten thousand workers out of a job.

In the same year, 1878, the joiners of Manchester, together with those of other Lancashire towns, applied for an increase from $8\frac{1}{2}$d to 10d an hour. They also wanted a reduction of hours from fifty-two to forty-nine and a half. When their claim was rejected, a prolonged struggle ensued lasting twelve months. In spite of the full support of the Council, the men were defeated and had to return to work at the old rate.

Arbitration Courts

In May, 1868, the Council approached the Manchester Chamber of Commerce to set up a local Court of Arbitration to which industrial disputes could be taken. The Manchester Free Labour Association, an organisation of blacklegs formed to break strikes, tried to get representation on the Court, but Lord Egerton Chairman of the Chamber of Commerce refused to support them. Although the Court was formally set up, the Secretary of the Trades Council reported in 1876 that it had never had a case to adjudicate.

The Council at Work

One of the first meetings organised by the Council in 1867 was in the Free Trade Hall.

It was a gathering of trades unionists called to denounce the Sheffield Outrages. These so called outrages were not, however, confined to Sheffield. Manchester Brickmakers also opposed the use of machinery in their trade and took drastic action against non-unionists acting as blacklegs. The Government pontificated in its most pompous manner and referred in its inquiry to, "Acts of intimidation, outrage and wrong promoted or encouraged or contrived at by Trade Unions in Manchester and its neighbourhood." [5] At the Free Trade Hall meeting, the audience of six thousand sent a telegram to the London Trades meeting the same evening. It read, "A great indignation meeting of the trades and working men of Manchester is now being held in the Free Trade Hall condemnatory of the Sheffield Trade outrages. Upwards of 6,000 present in Hall and as many outside. Great excitement prevails. The speakers are all working men. The men of Manchester are doing their duty. They denounce outrage but will stand by their unions." [6]

The First Trade Union Congress

The Manchester Trades Council was responsible for the circular dated 21st February, 1868, which called together the national conference of trades unions which became the Trades Union Congress. The conference was held in the Mechanics Institute in David Street, Manchester, during Whit Week, from 2nd to 6th June. W.H. Wood was elected President, F. Booker of Salford Amalgamated Society of Carpenters and Joiners, Vice President, and Peter Shorrocks, Secretary.

21

Peter Shorrocks

Peter Shorrocks was a tailor who had played an active and significant part in the formation of a National Society of Tailors. Under his leadership, the Manchester Tailors' Society called a conference on 12th March, 1866, where sixty-seven Societies with sixty thousand members were represented. From this conference, the Amalgamated Society of Tailors was formed with its Headquarters in Manchester. In January, 1867, Shorrocks succeeded in carrying through an amalgamation with the London Society of Tailors. This considerably strengthened the Union and brought Shorrocks into contact with the International Working Mens' Association, which had given assistance to London Tailors during their strike in 1866. The London Society was affiliated to the International.

The new Tailors' Union was soon involved in a sharp clash with the employers involving a prolonged lock out in Manchester. Shorrocks was summoned for conspiracy. Sergeant Balentine, leading Council for the Masters, claimed that picketting was illegal, being a form of intimidation. He also contended that by combining to prevent the employers from obtaining workers, the leaders were guilty of conspiracy. Shorrocks was acquitted but some of his colleagues were found guilty and one of them, Knox, was sentenced to three months imprisonment. At the first Trades Union Congress, Shorrocks read a paper on the law relating to conspiracy and picketting, calling on these experiences to illustrate his points. The conference declared the law to be unjust and called for its repeal. To act as mentor and guide,

Shorrocks was elected to the Parliamentary Committee.

The International Working Mens' Association

In February, 1868, Shorrocks wrote to the General Council of the IWMA and volunteered assistance in persuading unions in Manchester to affiliate to it. In October of that year, he took a hundred copies of the IWMA Congress Report and undertook to circulate a letter giving details of the New York, U.S.A., paper stainers' strike.

From the formation of the Trades Council, Shorrocks had been on the Executive Committee. At the fourth Annual Meeting of the Trades Council, held on October 11th, 1870, in the Stanley Arms, Broughton Road, Salford, Shorrocks persuaded the Council to adopt a resolution which read, "This Council entertains the opinion that we accord the International Working Mens' Association our moral support in all its various undertakings throughout the whole industrial world."[7]

When a Branch of the IWMA was formed in Manchester in the Autumn of 1871, Shorrocks became an active member of it. On 18th September, 1872, he was a delegate from Salford IWMA Branch to the Manchester Federal Council and at the Council meeting on November 27th, 1872, he was elected to the Chair.

The International in Manchester declined and the Salford Branch became a Republican Club. On 23rd September, 1873, Shorrocks addressed this Club in Ford Street Temperance Hall on the subject, "Republicanism or Royalty".

When W.H. Wood gave up the Secretaryship

of the Trades Council in 1877, Shorrocks was
elected to the position.

References

[1] The Times, 3rd June 1867.

[2] W. J. Davis, The British Trades Union Congress, History and Recollections, Vol. 1, 1910, p. 138.

[3] The Reverend James Fraser, M. A., Bishop of Manchester, member of the Commission on the Employment of Children, Young Persons and Women in Agriculture, 1867.

[4] Pomona Gardens was where Pomona Docks now is.

[5] The Full Report of the Inquiry into any Acts of Intimidation, Outrage or Wrong etc., Manchester (ND 1868).

[6] The Times, 3rd June 1867.

[7] Documents of the First International 1870-1871. Vol. 4 (ND) p. 90. Reports in "The Beehive" and "Manchester City News" omit reference to this resolution. One can only assume it was moved by Shorrocks.

Chapter 3

The New Unionism, 1880-1900.

"In our hands is placed the power
greater than their hoarded gold;
Greater than the might of armies,
magnified a thousandfold,
We can bring to birth a new world
from the ashes of the old,
For the Union makes us strong."

Solidarity Forever!

Ralph Chaplin.

The long depression from 1873 to 1896
marked the end of Britain's industrial monopoly
of the world market. Slumps in 1879/80, 1885/87
and 1891/93, gave rise to unemployment on a scale
unknown during the 1850's and 1860's, with the
exception of the Lancashire Cotton Famine of
1862/63. These factors affected the development
of the working class movement and contributed
towards political changes that heralded the new
century.

In the 1880's, the majority of delegates to the
Trades Council supported the Liberal Party.
Peter Shorrocks had gravitated towards Liberalism
but his days as Secretary of the Council were
numbered. He died in 1885, and relinquished his
office some time before that possibly due to ill
health. He was succeeded as Secretary by G.D.
Kelly, who took over in 1883.

Kelly had been elected full time Secretary of
the Amalgamated Society of Lithographic Printers
in 1879. He took office in January, 1880, and held

it until December, 1911. Kelley was a Liberal. He had been a delegate to the Council from 1871. He was Secretary of the Lithographic Printers and a member of the Parliamentary Committee of the Trades Union Congress. He was a member of the General Council of the Manchester Liberal Association. Another Liberal, Slatter, was the first working man to be appointed as a Magistrate on 21st May, 1885. He was also the first working representative to be elected to the local School Board in 1879. Other Liberals on the Council included, James Maudsley, the leader of the cotton spinners. He later became a Conservative. During the years he was a delegate to the Council, from 1880 to 1890, he supported the Liberal Party. In 1882, he was a member of the Parliamentary Committee of the T. U. C. , and in 1885 he contested the Bradford Ward in the City Council Elections. By 1895, however, he was an avowed Conservative and stood for Parliament both then and in 1906. The President of the Council between 1886 and 1895, Matthew Arrandale, the General Secretary of the United Machine Workers also contested a City Council seat as a Liberal. He stood in 1891, but was unsuccessful.

During the 1880's, the affairs of the Council were at a low ebb. In 1881, the 'Balance in Hand' dropped from £26 to £16. Only thirty-five Branches were affiliated and many Unions were unrepresented. The Council called a conference to discuss organisation and the ways by which it could be strengthened. A few years later, in 1884, affiliated membership had increased by four hundred. These were, of course, mainly the 'skilled' trades. Up to this time, few unions organising labourers or unskilled workers were admitted. In 1885, an important step was taken when quarterly meetings were replaced by monthly.

The Trades Council recognised the importance and significance of the adoption of the Manchester Ship Canal Act. On 3rd October, 1885, it organised a demonstration in which fifty-two Societies were represented by thirty thousand workers. It was a colourful and imaginative occasion. The Boilermakers and Shipbuilders carried a model of a large screw steamer. Three thousand engineers carried their trade emblems. The tin-plate workers made a suit of armour for their standard bearer. This was much admired. The glass workers flourished glass swords and many wore glass helmets. The Bookbinders held aloft an enormous tome and the press reported a "successful and colourful demonstration." [1]

Although the Council continued to represent the "pompous trades" and to uphold the banner of Liberalism, a new force was developing which was to have a considerable impact. This was Socialism. In 1883, a pamphlet, "Socialism Made Plain" was written by Henry Hyndman and published anonymously. From that time the new cause made slow but steady progress. One of the first local Socialists was William Horrocks. He was a turner and a member of the Salford Branch of the Amalgamated Society of Engineers. He joined the Salford Branch of the Social Democratic Federation, which had been formed on the initiative of Henry Musgrave Reid in 1884. The Branch remained small for a number of years, but eventually it started to grow and its members helped to activate the burst of trade union activity in the last decade of the century. It was mainly the Socialists who, from the beginning of 1889, began the task of organising the unskilled workers.

In Salford, the gas workers were dissatisfied with the twelve-hour shifts they had been working. They sent a deputation to the Salford Branch of the Social Democratic Federation (SDF), asking for assistance in forming a union. In September, 1889, the Salford Branch of the Gasworkers and General Labourers' Union was formed, with Bill Horrocks as Secretary. Among other aims were an eight-hour day and payment for working overtime. The Socialists, George Evans, George Tabbron and William Horrocks, visited the towns around Manchester recruiting to the union and succeeded in forming Branches of the Gasworkers Union. In 1890, there was a strike in support of the claim for an eight-hour day without reduction in pay. More than a thousand gas workers in Manchester and Salford were dismissed and many of them were not reinstated when the strike ended. The campaign did not end there, but continued throughout the 1890's.

The Association of Tramway and Vehicle Workers was formed by members of the Socialist League, a breakaway group from the SDF, led by William Morris. Tram guards worked sixteen hours a day, and decided that they should reduce them. The Socialist League members, Alf Barton and William Bailie, assisted the Carters and in 1889, the Manchester and Salford General Union of Carters was formed. A Branch of the Platelayers and General Railway Labourers' Union was also formed.

In 1890, William Johnson helped the Shop Workers to form a Branch of the United Shop Assistants' Union. Johnson, who was born in Yorkshire in 1866, had worked in textile mills in the United States and had been an organiser for the American Knights of Labour. When he returned to England, he worked as a shop assistant and was elected Secretary of the National Union of Shop Assistants when it was formed in 1891. He was also a foundation member of the Manchester and Salford Independent Labour Party.

The navvies constructing the Ship Canal were an obvious group needing organisation. Their long hours and atrocious conditions of work were notorious. Leonard Hall and John Wood organised them into the Navvies' and General Labourers' Union in 1890. Hall had a spectacular career. He was educated by his father, a doctor in Burnley. He also attended the Wesleyan Board School for a time. When he was thirteen, he went to work as a parcel lad at Burnley Railway Station for seven shillings a week. The following year he travelled steerage to the United States where he became, in turn, a sailor, soldier and cowboy. He agitated against the Virginia Oyster Skippers League and was found almost dead in a Carolina swamp. After working his way back to England on a cattle boat, he became one of the leaders of the London unemployed. Hall is described as, "Born a rebel, trouble gathered inevitably about his head, and he bowed not to it, but fought gaily with a clear brain, some skill as an administrator and a powerful gift for playing on the heart-strings of the mob." [2] When he became Lancashire District Secretary of the Navvies'

Bricklayers and General Labourers' Union, he organised not only navvies, but also yarn dyers, railway signalmen, railway porters, foundrymen and general labourers.

G. D. Kelley commented on these developments from the Olympian height of the craft unionist. He was reported as saying that he did not think "the New Unionism would last long" and that the eight-hour day was "impossible in application in all trades." [3]

The New Unionism did last, however, and had a profound effect on the whole Trade Union Movement. The decline in membership of the craft unions was reversed, some unions doubling or even trebling their pre-1889 figures. The Trades Council also grew. In 1880, it had thirty affiliated Societies, while in 1890 it had doubled to sixty. In March, 1891, Kelley stated that when he had taken over the Secretaryship of the Council there had been sixteen delegates connected with it. "There are now 108", he said, "and almost every skilled trade in Manchester and Salford is enrolled in its ranks... we have at present numerous applications from unskilled workers, such as railway navvies, gas labourers and ship canal workers, whom I presume we shall admit, but we have not yet decided." [4] The Trades Council did accept the affiliations of unskilled workers' unions and the wind of change penetrated its deliberations.

In 1892, a move was made to organise a United May Day Demonstration for the first time in Manchester. London had shown the way the previous year. A number of Unions decided to join forces with the Socialist Societies and on Sunday, 1st May, Manchester workers assembled in Stevenson's Square hours before the march was

31

due to set off. Leonard Hall, then aged twenty-six, rode at the head of the procession on a white horse in front of a white ensign embroidered with the words "Work For All, Overtime For None". Behind him marched the Manchester Fabians, the Railwaymen with their banner, "Unity is Strength". The Tailors, the Bakers and Confectioners, the Spindle and Fly Makers followed. The Dressers, Dyers and Finishers banner called for "Equality By Right, Justice For All". Behind them were the Horsehair and Fibre Workers and the men of the Navvies' and Bricklayers' Union. The scene was vividly described by Laurence Thompson:

"Twelve bands broke up the mass into companies, which marched six deep through the great throng of working people lining Oldham Street and Piccadilly. The women cried 'Bravo!' as the procession passed, and the men stamped their clogs, and spat, and wondered. There was a halt while the procession from Salford came into line. Then there were only the bands and the banners to keep up their spirits as they marched through the silent respectable crowds in Portland Street and Oxford Road. But as they reached their own land, the long grey vista of the Stretford Road, they were met with cheer upon cheer from men, women and children swarming out of the wretched cottages and the narrow courts. There were cries of delight for each brave slogan, for the coloured banners and the bands, and the crowd fell in behind, singing and laughing and chattering as if England had risen at last and the long, long night was really over.

Into Alexandra Park they went, where the buds were bursting on the trees, and the sun shone, and the Police stood stolidly about the six platforms.

32

There were Comrade Sidney Webb of the London County Council, and Don Roberto, Cunninghame Graham, with his pointed beard and his silver wit, looking as if he had just stepped from a Velasquez painting, William Johnson, the dashing Prince Rupert who commanded the Shop Assistants' Union, the little fighting cock Alfred Settle, Horsfall of the Workmen's Times staff, and half a dozen more. They spoke and the crowds cheered. No matter what they said, the crowds cheered, for it was May-day, and the banners curled bravely in the wind.

Blatchford was Chairman at the first platform, a covered cart like a camel's cage, through the bars of which he smiled his heart out upon the happy crowd. He had a headache and a bad cold, and no-one heard his speech except the Police. But when he cried, 'Hands up for Socialism!' every hand was raised. Before nightfall, between sixty thousand and a hundred thousand working men and women had committed themselves to demanding nationalisation of the land, an eight-hour day, payment of M. P. s, shorter Parliaments, adult suffrage and an independent Labour Party.

Upon John Trevor's initiative, Blatchford called a few days later to form a Manchester and Salford Independent Labour Party. It was able at once to enrol almost seven hundred members. May-day had been a triumph indeed." [5]

The Trades Council had decided not to organise the 1892 Labour Day by a narrow majority. When the issue was raised in 1893, it gave rise to a sharp clash. At first the Council decided to participate, but when Leonard Hall moved that the I. L. P. should be represented on the organising committee, it was strongly opposed by G. D. Kelley on the grounds that the object of the I.L.P. was to defeat Liberal candidates and thus to bolster up the Conservative Party. He offered to prove that I.L.P. funds could be traced to Tory businessmen and he appealed to delegates not to allow politics to creep into trade unionism. The debate continued during three meetings. In reply, Leonard Hall was reported as saying, "Mr. Kelley had so long accustomed himself to the view that the Council had been permanently 'nobbled' for the Liberal Party that... he regarded any attempt to shake off the old monopoly as mere presumption." He rather unkindly went on to quote Kelley's Presidential Address to the Leicester Electoral Congress, "Labour questions have been shelved by both sides of Parliament." This indifference, he maintained, "had created a party comprising no inconsiderable section of the workers of this country... a Labour Party, pure and simple."[6] A resolution was put to the Council suggesting that as there was such a divergence of views, the decision to take part in the Labour Day Demonstration should be rescinded "as damaging to the interests of the Council."[7] This was passed by sixty-three votes to twenty-seven.

The I.L.P. decided to go ahead with the arrangements in spite of the Trades Council's withdrawal and the Demonstration was held with the support of the Amalgamated Society of Railway Servants, the General Railway Workers' Union, the Painters' Society, the Labour Amalgamation, the Amalgamated Society of Carpenters, the India Rubber Workers, the Cotton Operatives, the Dressers, Dyers and Finishers, the Gasworkers, the Mat Makers, the Enginemen and Firemen, the Tailors' Society, the Jewish Tailors and the

Cloggers Society. Robert Blatchford, Editor of
The Clarion, wrote, "Manchester Labour Day
of 1893 was something more than a success; it
was a triumph... the attendance was enormous,
and the steady earnestness and quiet dignity of
the twenty thousand 'persons of no repute' who
formed the procession, constituted not only a
panegyric upon the Labour Party, but a scathing
satire upon the fussy impotencies and nervous
futilities which did so much to make authority
ridiculous." Blatchford asked what justification
there was for "the presence of a lot of half drilled
constables on horseback, armed with swords and
pistols." He went on to question when and "under
what circumstances were these weapons to be
used?"[8].

When the election to the Executive Committee
took place, two Socialists, George Tabbron of the
Manchester Brassfounders and Finishers and a
member of the S. D. F., and J. Harker, an I. L. P.
member of the Shirt, Jacket and Cutters' Society
were elected. The other nine members of the
E. C. were Liberals or Conservatives. During
1894, the Council changed its name to the
Manchester and Salford Trades and Labour Council
and actively campaigned on behalf of the unemployed
workers.

The Council called a conference during 1894
which was attended by delegates from the I. L. P.,
the Voluntary Organising Committee of the A. S. E.,
and the Building Federation of Manchester and
Salford. The conference drew up a Labour
Programme which included demands for equal pay
for equal work irrespective of sex and for a national
incremental scale for teachers.

The experience of the two May Day demonstrations

had changed the attitude of many of the Council delegates and when the decision as to whether the Council should participate in 1895 was put to the vote, forty-one were in favour of doing so and forty-two against. To understand the situation it is necessary to look at the most prominent members of the Council and see where their affiliations lay. The Liberal members included, G.D. Kelly of the Litho-printers, M. Arrandale, United Machine Workers, E.E. Roberts, Bookbinders and Machine Rulers. The Conservative interest was supported by F. Entwistle of the A.S.E. The Socialists included I.L.P. members, Leonard Hall of the General Labourers' Union, J. Harker of the Shirt and Jacket Cutters' Society, J.E. Sutton of the Bradford Miners, J. Nuttall, Block Roller and Stamp Cutters, J.E. Hart, Portmanteau Makers and J. Billam of the Upper Mersey Water-men and Porters' Association, while the S.D.F. was represented by George Tabbron of the Brass-founders. When, in 1895, the number of Socialists on the Executive Committee was raised to five out of the nine, a decision was taken to organise the May Day Demonstration. This was the first of many that the Trades Council organised during the next half century.

The march in 1895 went to Peel Park, and resolutions were passed calling for, "a national Federation of all Trades and Labour Organisations, for the purpose of successfully coping with the changed conditions introduced into our industrial struggles by Federated Capital" and for "Independent Representation of Labour on all legislative and adminstrative bodies."[9]   An eight-hour day and nationalisation of the land were also agreed upon in

MANCHESTER AND SALFORD TRADES AND LABOUR COUNCIL.

Report and Balance Sheet

OF THE

MAY-DAY DEMONSTRATION COMMITTEE,
1898.

FELLOW-WORKERS,

The decision of the Trades Council to take the initiative in organising this year's Demonstration resulted in a larger number of trade unions taking part than in previous years, and materially assisted in bringing about a better understanding and closer union amongst the trade unions and other labour organisations. It is to be hoped that this spirit will continue to be fostered in the future, and thus give to the Annual Demonstration that united and representative character which the cause of labour demands.

Twenty-six trade unions, the Independent Labour Party, the Social Democratic Federation, and the Manchester Labour Church, took part in the Demonstration, which was acknowledged to be the largest in point of numbers and the most successful May-Day Labour Demonstration yet held.

The Corporations of Manchester and Salford rendered every assistance to the Committee for successfully carrying out the Demonstration, and the arrangements made by the respective Corporations at Albert Square, Peel Park, and along the route of the procession, were excellent.

Meetings were addressed at Peel Park, Salford, by over forty speakers from five platforms, and resolutions dealing with important labour and social questions were unanimously adopted. A copy of the resolutions are appended to this Report.

The Committee are pleased to report that the expenses of the Demonstration have been more than covered by the income received, thus leaving a small balance for next year's Demonstration.

F. ENTWISTLE, J.P., CHAIRMAN.

J. NUTTALL, DEMONSTRATION SECRETARY.

Manchester and Salford Trades and Labour Council

ESTABLISHED  1866.

Place of Meeting:
St. James Schoolroom, Major Street,

63, Upper Brook Street,

MANCHESTER, *July 27th, 1897.*

DEAR SIRS,

The following resolution has been passed by the Manchester and Salford Trades and Labour Council:—**"That this Council, recognising the importance of the struggle the Amalgamated Society of Engineers and Kindred Trades have entered upon, and its value to the whole of the workers of this country, pledges itself to do its utmost to win the battle. Fully recognising the altered conditions and methods of modern industrial warfare, we earnestly recommend to the consideration of the Trade Unionists of Great Britain the advisability of being prepared with financial help."**

The E.C. of the Council, in submitting this resolution, feel that the present dispute is so unique in character involving issues of great importance to the workers of the whole country, and that a spontaneous expression of practical sympathy with those engaged in the contest in anticipating the inevitable strain upon the funds of the societies implicated will be of the utmost value at the present juncture. If the fight is to be won, and as men and trades unionists we cannot discuss the alternative, it is the duty of all who live by labour to assist at once both morally and financially those who have been forced into the present conflict, and we have every confidence that this will be done to the fullest extent. As the dispute may be a prolonged one, the E.C. would suggest that the affiliated societies should arrange for a **Weekly Contribution, however small**, in preference to a lump sum; the proceeds to be forwarded to the Treasurer of the Council, Mr. Councillor R. W. WATTERS, at 19, Hayfield Terrace, Seedley; or to the Secretary, Mr. GEO. D. KELLEY, 63, Upper Brook Street, Chorlton-on-Medlock. All monies forwarded will be distributed under the direction of the E.C. of the Council.

On behalf of the Council,

Yours fraternally,

F. ENTWISTLE, J.P., President.
Councillor R. W. WATTERS, Treasurer.
GEO. D. KELLEY, J.P., Secretary.

principle. To meet the unemployment position, Manchester and Salford Corporations were asked to introduce an eight-hour day and to carry out public work by direct employment of labour.

Aid to Workers in Dispute
Among many disputes of the later years of the century, the Engineers' Lock-out in 1897 was outstanding. It lasted for seven months and the Council decided to "pledge itself to do its utmost to win the battle."[10]   Circulars were sent out and deputations visited affiliated unions with considerable success. When the Manchester District Allied Trades Joint Committee presented its Balance Sheet on 11th June, 1898, it reported that £6,462 had been raised apart from the money sent by Unions to their General Office. The efforts of the Trades Council were particularly praised.

International Affairs
The extent to which the outlook of the Council had broadened was shown in 1896, when representatives were sent to the International Socialist, Workers and Trade Union Congress held in London. Following the Congress, a Reception Committee wrote to the Council asking them to cooperate with the S.D.F. in organising a meeting on May 31st at the Free Trade Hall to be addressed by the German Socialist, Wilhelm Liebknecht. After sonciderable discussion, it was agreed to send six representatives from the Trades Council.
The following year, the Council discussed distress in India and the view was adopted that "the most populous empire that the world had known, under British rule was on the brink of an

unprecedented economic and social collapse."
Two hundred and fifty million people "for whose
welfare the British Government were responsible,
were in the midst of a famine" growing daily
worse. The resolution passed by the Council
expressed the "strong conviction" that the famine
was caused by the "maladministration of the
affairs of India by our present and previous
Government" and further that it had been brought
about by a "deliberate policy of greed and
oppression". The Council's conviction, however
justified and indeed borne out by subsequent events,
had no effect on the Government. The British
ruling class was determined to exploit India as
"the brightest jewel in the Imperial Crown." [11]
It was from this intense exploitation of the colonial
people that the ruling class could offer crumbs to
British workers and so allay their more dangerous
discontent.

Interest in international affairs continued. In
1898, the Council sent out an appeal from the
London Trades Council asking for aid for political
prisoners in Italy and in the last year of the century
a protest was made against British troops being
sent to the Transvaal.

References

[1] Manchester Guardian, 5th October, 1885.

[2] Laurence Thompson, Robert Blatchford: Portrait of an Englishman, p. 88.

[3] Workman's Times, 5th September, 1890.

[4] Manchester Faces and Places, 10th March, 1891.

[5] Laurence Thompson, op. cit., pp. 86-7.

[6] The Clarion, 13th May, 1893.

[7] Arthur Woollerton, The Labour Movement in Manchester and Salford, p. 10.

[8] The Clarion, 13th May, 1893.

[9] Manchester and Salford Trades and Labour Council, 31st Annual Report, 1897.

[10] ibid.

[11] ibid.

Chapter 4

Organising Women

"As we come marching, marching,
  we battle too, for men,
For they are women's children and
  we mother them again.
Our lives shall not be sweated from
  birth until life closes.
Hearts starve as well as bodies:
Give us bread, but give us roses."

Bread and Roses,

James Oppenheim.

Manchester has been the centre of a number
of attempts to allow women equal opportunities to
serve their own and their families' interests. By
the nature of the industry which developed in the
area, Lancashire women went to work away from
home as soon as the factories were built to
accommodate them. Women at times of
unemployment were often the breadwinners and
girls were brought up to go to work as soon as
they were able. It is no accident that Mrs. Mary
Fildes sat next to Henry Hunt on the cart which
served as a platform when the Manchester men
and women met, to demand the right to
representation in Parliament, in St. Peter's
Fields on August 16th, 1819. Samuel Bamford
tells how he invited women to participate in the
meetings to discuss the reform of Parliament and
there were a number of Female Reformers'
Societies before the 1832 Reform Act. The part
which women played in the struggles of the

nineteenth century tends to be obscured. The Preston strike of 1854, for example, is a story of solidarity throughout the County. Collections poured into Preston to support the strikers. Much of it must have been sent by women workers because the work force in the textile industry was largely female. Of the twenty thousand (at a conservative estimate) strikers, a proportion must have been women, but they are lost in the general term 'cotton operatives'.

One of the earliest attempts to provide trade union protection specifically for women was in 1874, when Mrs. Emma Paterson formed the Women's Trade Union League and it was probably their letter which was read in correspondence to the Manchester and Salford Trades Council in October, 1888, asking for help in organising Manchester women workers.

Some of the worst conditions were in the tailoring trade and meetings were held to try to interest the women in their own welfare. A new society was formed which was open to machinists, tailoresses and mantle makers. Soon it had nearly seventy members. The following year, 1889, the Trades Council intervened for the first time on behalf of women workers at the Manchester Cigarette Factory. The Manchester Examiner reported that although the Trades Council sent a delegation to the factory, no progress was made and the girls returned to work at the old rate. In 1890, the Trades Council continued its efforts and tried to organise the women in the waterproof garment trades. They came on a snag which often beset those who tried to help women to help themselves. They found that the women so lacked confidence in their own

41

power that they feared the sack more than the appalling conditions under which they were working. They did not attend meetings lest they be discharged. So many factors affect a woman's thinking, lack of mobility, the traditional role as wife and mother, and the desire of many men to keep their wives in a state of subjugation. The battle to develop women's confidence in themselves has not even yet been won.

The Trades Council, however, continued its efforts. When Lady Dilkie, President of the Women's Trade Union League, visited Manchester to try to promote the organisation of women's unions, the Trades Council promised every assistance. In 1892, public meetings were held, circulars were sent out appealing for funds and the Council decided to appoint a woman organiser. This woman, whose identity is lost, spent eleven weeks going from workshop to workshop distributing thousands of leaflets and trying to contact the women workers. It was two and a half years before any notable progress was made.

At a meeting held in the Mayor's Parlour on 1st February, 1895, a group of men and women mainly connected with the Liberal Party decided to form a Women's Trade Union Council to cover the Manchester and Salford District. It was sponsored by the Trades Council. Two full-time women organisers were appointed. One was Sarah Welsh, who later as Mrs. Sarah Dickenson continued to act as Secretary of the Council until 1901, when she was joined by Eva Gore Booth. She continued to be actively associated with the work until the merger with the Trades Council in 1918. Although little is known about Sarah Welsh, it is probable that she was born in 1868 and went to school for a few years until

she started work in a factory in 1879. She
continued working until she accepted the
responsibility of the Secretaryship of the newly
formed Women's Trades Union Council in 1895.
She was one of the few working women who were
involved in the formation of the Council.

Miss Esther Roper was a key figure in the
establishment of the Council. She was a graduate
of Owen's College and took her B.A. in 1891.
She realised that since so many of the established
trades unions refused to admit women, separate
organisation had to be provided for them. Her
interest in working women stemmed from her
association with the movement to obtain the vote.
When she left the University she became Secretary
of the North of England Society for Women's
Suffrage. Her attitude that the questions of women's
welfare and organisation were inextricably mixed
with the fight for the vote was not always accepted
by the Council and later led to a split.

In 1895, after she had been working with the
Council for a year, Miss Roper went to a friend's
house in Bordighera in Italy. There she met a
young Irish woman who was recuperating from
consumption. She was "tall and excessively slender,
intensely short sighted, with a mass of golden hair,
worn like a great ball at the nape of her long neck,
bespectacled, bending forward, short of breath with
high-pitched voice and gasping speech."[1] This
was Eva Gore Booth, the third child of an Irish
baronet who had a sympathy with the peasants.
In times of stress, Sir Henry gave out meal to his
starving tenants and his children helped him. Eva
was widely read and had a passion for beauty. She
had achieved some reputation as a poet. The two
young women walked and talked much in the course

43

of the weeks they were together and the result
was that Eva returned with her friend to live in
Manchester. She thought she was dying of T.B.
and determined to devote her remaining time to
the cause of the working women of Manchester.
Fortunately she was mistaken in her diagnosis.

The Gore Booth family had owned land in
Salford for generations and her cousin held the
family living there. In 1897 she settled in
Manchester and devoted her time to activity
among working women in both the trade union and
political movements. In 1900 she was appointed
co-secretary with Sarah Dickenson, of the
Manchester and Salford Women's Trade Union
Council. The main object of the Council was to
form trade unions catering specifically for women
workers. The two women became close friends
and their combined work was instrumental in
building the women's movement in Manchester.
Mrs. Dickenson wrote of Eva Gore Booth, "my
first impression of her was her charming and
interesting personality. When I knew her better
I found how very genuine she was in all her
dealings and discovered all the beautiful traits in
her character. The friendly way that she treated
all the women Trade Unionists endeared her to them.
If she was approached for advice or help she never
failed. She is remembered by thousands of working
women in Manchester for her untiring efforts to
improve their industrial conditions, for awakening
and educating their sense of political freedom, and
for social intercourse."[2]

During her sixteen years in Manchester, Miss
Gore Booth represented women workers on the
Manchester Education Committee. She worked at
the University Settlement and formed a dramatic

society with a group of sixteen extremely rough girls who readily responded to her "patience and love". Early Sunday mornings she took a reading class at the Ancoats Brotherhood, where the reading of a classic such as Shelley's poems was followed by discussion led by Eva. During all this time she continued writing poetry and plays. In the early years of the century, Esther Roper and Eva Gore Booth met the Pankhurst family and their work for womens' suffrage was intensified. By 1913, Eva's health could no longer stand the Lancashire climate, and she had to live in the South, where she died in June, 1926, just after the General Strike.

The Manchester Women's Trades Union Council made its first major break-through in May, 1896, when the 'Manchester and Salford Society of Women Employed in the Bookbinding and Printing Trades' was formed. It flourished for forty-six years before merging with the National Union. During the whole of its existence, the Secretary was Isabel Forsyth. She started work at the age of thirteen in a printing works for the wage of 3s. 6d. a week. After five years she was getting 12s. for a $52\frac{1}{2}$ hour week. When she was made full-time secretary of the newly formed union, she said that if she could achieve a thousand members and £1 a week wages for the girls she would die happy. The £1 was reached in 1917 and the membership then crept up to two and a half thousand. But, at the end of her first year of office, it only stood at one hundred and thirty five. The first contributions were two pence a week and during the year the income was £42. After paying working expenses, £5 in sickness benefit and £3 in unemployment pay, the Society ended the year with a balance of £30. The growth of the Union was

largely due to the energy and enthusiasm of Miss
Forsyth, who visited workshops in her dinner hour
and held impromptu meetings with the girls. In
1908 she was appointed full-time Secretary. While
working part-time as Union Official and part-time
at the trade, Miss Forsyth had been paid 10/- a
quarter.

The original Women's Trade Union Council
consisted of sixty-eight members, of whom only
twenty were trade unionists and only four of them
were women, from the Federation of Women
Workers, a sick and benefit society that had been
set up in 1889. The Executive Committee had
seventeen members, of whom eight were men and
nine women. The Liberals gave firm support from
the start and Councillor Arrandale was Vice-
Chairman of the E.C.. By 1901, the number of
women on the E.C. had increased to eleven.
During the early years, the income was mainly
derived from provate donations. Out of an income
of £260, only £21 was given by trades unions. The
objects of the Council were:-

"1 To promote new and encourage existing
organisations among women workers.

2 To collect and publish information as to
conditions under which women work,
with a view to influencing public opinion
and promoting legislation for the
improvement of their conditions of labour.

3 To endeavour by all legitimate means
to improve such conditions by
obtaining for women workers fair
and uniform wages, shorter hours,
and sanitary workrooms."[3]

Difficulties beset the path of the Council from the first. Women lacked confidence and experience and were easily discouraged. A group of umbrella makers numbering eighty when it was formed, was reduced to seven in 1897, thirty being lost at one works where the Foreman brought pressure to bear on them. During a quarter of a century the Women's Trade Union Council helped to bring into being forty new trade unions or branches of existing unions. Organisers were sent as far afield as Rotherham, Birmingham, Bolton and Sheffield to try to assist women to organise. The trades which the Council succeeded in organising were, tailoresses, cap makers, india rubber workers, fancy box makers, chair makers, shirt makers, cigarette makers, midwives, cafe workers, typists and female shippers.

The Council showed considerable interest in the organisation of women both nationally and internationally. In 1899, Mrs. Marland Brodie reported at the International Conference of Women in London, "The Manchester Women's Trades Union Council is doing excellent work in that vicinity."[4] The delegate to the Conference from Manchester was Miss Ashwell. She contributed to the discussion and said, that the experience of the Council among non-textile workers of Manchester was that comparatively small bodies of women could by careful negotiation with the employers gain definite improvements in wages. She advocated trades unionism for all women because, she pointed out, the poorest and most down-trodden were most in need. She had seen unskilled women earning 8s. a week organised and succeed in gaining an advance of wages. The task of organising working women she said was difficult, "but it was thoroughly practicable and urgently necessary."[5]

The early years of the century were marked by a great increase in the interest shown in the cause of women's enfranchisement. In 1901, Christabel Pankhurst became acquainted with Esther Roper and Eva Gore Booth. She began to join in the activities of the Manchester Women's Suffrage Society of which Esther Roper was Secretary. Her mother and sister Sylvia became interested in her work. In 1901 a petition signed by sixty seven thousand textile workers was taken to the House of Commons to demand the vote for women. At many of the meetings where the petition was presented, a vote was taken as to whether the question of women's suffrage should become a trade union question and in each case it was carried by large majorities. The petition was organised by Eva Gore Booth, Esther Roper and Miss Reddish, herself a textile worker.

At a meeting called by Mrs. Pankhurst at her home at 62, Nelson Street, on 10th October, 1903, the Women's Social and Political Union was formed. Almost all the women who were present on that occasion were working women. The phrase "Votes for Women" was adopted as the watchword for the new union.

The campaign that was waged by the newly formed group of active women among the trade unionists and workers led to a considerable amount of frustration. It seemed that there was much sympathy for the cause of women's suffrage but little inclination to demonstrate sincerity by producing results. The textile workers in July, 1904, agreed to form a Committee from Lancashire and Cheshire towns to campaign for a suitable candidate willing to support votes for women in Parliament. It was called 'The Lancashire and Cheshire Women's Textile and Other Workers Representation Committee'. Mr. Thorley Smith in Wigan was selected as the candidate and the women worked for him to such effect that he was returned second at the poll.

Christabel Pankhurst, Esther Roper and Eva Gore Booth worked together to achieve this result. Christabel became a member of the small organising committee of the Council and the three women went on holiday to Venice. Miss Pankhurst wrote, "I joined their respective committees and fought many a battle by their side, with a view to getting women's suffrage recognised as a question of urgent practical importance from the industrial point of view. This was a stage in my political apprenticeship of great and lasting value, and I owe much to the example and sympathy of these two friends."[6]

The difficulties that the Women's Trades Council had to contend with can be illustrated by the dispute that took place between the Northern Counties Weavers' Amalgamation and the Manchester and Salford Power Loom Weavers' Association, an all women union which had been set up under the auspices of the Women's Trade Union Council. There was an attempt at amalgamation of the two committees which failed because of a difference in the amount of contribution paid. After a lapse of time, the powerful Northern Counties Amalgamation approached the Manchester organisation again and suggested that the question be reconsidered. This time, the Manchester women claimed the right to appoint a woman Secretary and to have a woman representative on the Amalgamation Executive. The men in the

Amalgamation were horrified at the suggestion and set up a rival Manchester organisation. This split in the forces left both seriously weakened. For a number of years, the total number of women in the two Unions was less than the Manchester Power Loom Weavers had on its books before the dissension.

On the positive side, efforts made by the Council to get Eva Gore Booth elected on to the Technical Institute Committee of the Manchester City Council were successful in 1903. Through her, the women's Trade Union Council entered a strongly worded protest against the exclusion of girls from scholarships at the Municipal School of Technology. The Council took an interest in education and the welfare of children and as early as 1899 wrote to all the Lancashire Members of Parliament asking them to support the National Union of Teachers' Campaign to raise the legal age at which children could be employed, from eleven to twelve.

Esther Roper, who was the Secretary of the North of England Women's Suffrage Committee, had maintained from the formation of the Women's Trades Council that the questions of women's welfare and trad union rights could only be resolved when women had a say in running their affairs through representation in Parliament. The Council, which had been formed largely as the result of the activity of the Liberal Party in Manchester, found itself seriously split over questions involving direct political activity in the interest of votes for women. The Chairman of the Manchester and Salford Trades Council, Councillor M. Arrandale, J.P., and the Secretary, George Kelley, were both members of the Liberal Party. They and a number of middle class monied people had given financial support to the Council. When the suffrage campaign developed, they found themselves in disagreement with the women advocating political action on the Council. A paragraph in the Daily News in 1904, confused a leaflet written by Eva Gore Booth and published by the Women's Representation Committee with the Council's propaganda. This mistake was corrected by Miss Amy Bulley, the Chairman of the Council, and Eva Gore Booth. Miss Bulley also wrote a letter to the Manchester Guardian disclaiming any connection with the movement for the emancipation of women. She associated the Women's Trade Union Council with her remarks. Christabel Pankhurst immediately wrote to assure the readers that as a member of the Council she had to dissociate herself from the position taken by Miss Bulley. A special meeting of the Council was called to sort the matter out. Christabel Pankhurst moved a resolution urging the Council to bring their policy into line with that of the unions with which they were connected and take action to obtain political power for women. Letters were then read from a number of influential people who had supported the non-political policy of the Council. Among them were C.E. Schwann, M.P., James Johnston of the Independent Labour Party and H.V. Herford, the Treasurer. T.R. Marr also opposed Miss Pankhurst.

The Special Meeting was small. Only six people were present. The vote went against Christabel Pankhurst's resolution by four votes to two. Eva Gore Booth and Sarah Dickenson resigned from the Council and a number of unions wrote announcing their withdrawal. The number of women trade unionists fell from two thousand members to one hundred. Seven unions with a membership of two thousand women seceded from the Council and formed a new organisation, The Manchester and Salford Women's Trades and Labour Council. At the first

meeting on 29th September, 1904. Eva Gore
Booth and Sarah Dickenson were elected as joint
Secretaries.

Unfortunately, the records of the new
organisation have not survived. Esther Roper
described the activity up to the outbreak of war,
"The next ten years were full to overflowing with
organisation, writing, speaking at large
gatherings in all parts of England, deputations to
Cabinet Ministers and to Members of Parliament.
To this was added a new activity, when well-meant
and ill-meant efforts were made to restrict women's
labour in various fields. On different occasions,
women pit-brow workers, barmaids, women
acrobats and gymnasts, and women florists were
successfully organised in their own defence." [7]
For a time a paper called 'The Women's Labour
News' was edited by Eva Gore Booth. In her
editorial announcement in the first issue she said,
"Many are the difficult questions connected with
Labour, many are the misunderstandings and
confusions, many are the obscure corners of the
industrial world, and many are the wrongs done in
the darkness. Those who are working for the
betterment of political and industrial conditions of
women have great need of fellowship, of coherency
and free discussion, and the ventilation of pressing
grievances. The aim of this little paper is to light
a few street lamps here and there in the darkest
ways, to let us at all events see one another's faces
and recognise our comrades, and work together
with strong, organised and enlightened effort for
the uplifting of those who suffer most under the
present political and industrial system." [8]

The Objects of the new Trades and Labour
Council were:-

"1Discussion on all matters connected
with women's labour and joint action
of the federated unions for the
promotion of the industrial welfare
of the women workers.

2Formation of Trade Societies among
organised workers in any industry.

3Political action for the enfranchisement
of women workers."9

Among the unions that joined the new Trades
and Labour Council were the Manchester and
Salford Society of Women in the Bookbinding and
Printing Trades (established May 1896),
Manchester and Salford Power Loom Weavers
Association (est. 1903), Manchester and Salford
Ring Spinners and the Manchester and Salford
Patent Cop Winders, Bobbin and Hank Winders,
Gassers, Doublers, Reelers and Preparers.
During its existence, the new Council formed the
Prestwich Branch of the Co-operative Employees,
the National Union of Printing and Paper Workers,
the Manchester 4th Women's Guild Branch of the
National Union of Railwaymen and a women's
section of the National League of the Blind.
    Although there was a definite split that had
quite serious effects on the organisation of women,
both sides applied themselves to the necessary
work and in some cases there was obviously an
overlap. For example, the representative of the
Women's Trades Council at the National Labour
Conference on the State Maintenance of Children
on Friday, 20th January, 1905, about three months
after the split, was Mrs. D. Montefiore, well

53

known as an ardent and active suffragette and
Socialist. A year later, in October, 1905, the
Liberal President of the Men's Trades Council
moved a resolution at a meeting at the Free Trade
Hall, called to protest against the imprisonment
of Sylvia Pankhurst. His resolution, which was
seconded by Mrs. Dickenson, called for the
franchise for women on the same terms as for
men. It was obvious that the split quickly began
to heal and the way for the eventual reconciliation
was soon laid.

After the secession of the major unions to the
Trades and Labour Council in 1904, there were
only five unions left in the Women's Trades Council.
These were the Women Confectioners, the Sewing
Machinists, the Upholsterers and the Women's
Society of Fancy Leather Workers. The active
workers were Miss Amy Bulley, Chairman, Mr.
H. V. Herford, Treasurer, and Miss Emily Cox,
Secretary. Members of the Executive Committee
were, Councillor Kelley, Secretary of the Trades
Council, T. R. Marr from the University Settlement
and the Fabian Society, John Harker of the Trades
Council, the Labour Representation Committee and
the Shirt and Jacket Cutters Society, James
Johnston of the Independent Labour Party, Mrs.
Charles Schwann and Professor Tout. By 1907,
the Women's Trades and Labour Council had three
thousand affiliated members and the Women's
Trades Council had four hundred less. It also had
870 individual members.

By 1908, it was agreed to set up a joint
committee with the North of England Society for
Women's Suffrage. The tide of militant suffrage
activity was running so strongly that people began
to be swept up and carried along by it. The

Women's Trades Council agreed to join the Committee and take part in a demonstration but not to contribute to the expense. It is probable that they feared the loss of much of their income if they donated to a cause which was not acceptable to all the donors. Three members of the Council signed a petition to the Prime Minister asking for the inclusion of women in the promised franchise Bill. The petition was organised by the Women's Guild of Cooperators, and was signed by the three women as "officials but not on behalf of the Council."[10]   In 1910, the Women's Trades Council banner was carried in a suffrage demonstration in London.

In 1909, the first steps were taken to heal the split in the women's trade unions. A Joint Committee was set up with four men from the Trades Council, four women from the Trades and Labour Council and four women from the Women's Trades Council. This Committee was to consider effective organisation of women, and in 1910 it organised a joint demonstration to publicise trade unionism.

In 1908, a young Irish woman started work at the Clarion Cafe in Market Street. She became interested in the position of her fellow workers in the catering trade and pioneered trade union organisation in this field. She started work in Dublin, where her father was Secretary of the Brick and Stonemakers Union. He represented his Branch on the Dublin Trades Council. Mary Quaile was twenty-two when she came to Manchester and worked at the Clarion Cafe as a waitress and cook. Three years later, when she was twenty-five years old, she was appointed Assistant Organiser to the Manchester Women's Trades Council. She occupied this position from 1911 until 1914, when she was appointed the Organising Secretary. In April, 1919, after some months of negotiation, both the Women's Trades and Labour Council and the Women's Trades Council merged with the Manchester and Salford Trades Council, and Mary Quaile was appointed full-time Secretary to the Women's Group. In 1919, she was appointed Women's National Officer of the Dock and Riverside Worker's Union. She continued in this post when the Union amalgamated in 1921 to become the Transport and General Worker's Union. From 1923 until 1926 she was a member of the General Council of the Trades Union Congress. During this period she became a member of the International Committee of Women Trade Unionists. Her health compelled her to retire from full time work as a trade union official in 1933, but she had resumed her work with the Manchester and Salford Trades Council when she returned to Manchester in 1927 and again took office as Secretary of the Women's Group. In 1935, she was elected Vice-President of the Trades Council and from 1936 to 1958 she acted as Treasurer. The Trades Union Congress honoured her with the coveted T.U.C. Silver Badge, which was presented to her at a reception at Belle Vue where four thousand people had gathered to show their appreciation of her work.

After Mary Quaile took on the organising work of the Women's Trades Council, the drift to war accelerated and within a year or so the women's position had radically altered. Men were called to the armed Forces and women in much greater numbers went to work. Those men who remained at work realised that it was essential to organise the women if their hard won gains were not to be dissipated during the war. An upsurge of trade union activity among women took place. The nature of much of the work of the Women's Council changed to fit the unusual circumstances. Throughout the war years, two representatives from the Council sat on the Manchester Distress Committee formed to deal with cases of hardship caused by the war. When food prices began to rise in 1915, a Conference was called by The War Emergency Worker's National Committee. The Trades Council and the Women's Council together sponsored a Manchester Branch of this Committee. In 1916 it convened a Conference on the price of food and coal.

The Council took action in conjunction with the 'No Conscription Fellowship' and after delegates had attended the Conference in 1916 agreed to take part in propoganda against the Conscription Bill. Professor Tout resigned from the Council in protest. The wave of industrial unrest in 1917 which followed the deportation of the Clyde Shop Stewards involved the Women's Council. The Secretary gave evidence before the Commission on Industrial Unrest.

The story of the organisation of women in Manchester and Salford during the early years of the century reflects credit on all who participated. The men trade unionists gave support, both active and moral, to the efforts of the women themselves. In some ways, the women were the losers when they lost their identity in the Trades Council proper, but the history of the women's movement has always shown that real progress towards equality can only be made by men and women together − and that has not yet been fully achieved.

References

[1] The Woman Worker, 4th September, 1908. The Portrait Gallery, p. 347, J. J. Mallon.

[2] Poems of Eva Gore Booth – Complete Edition with Biographical Introduction by Esther Roper, 1929, p. 11.

[3] Women's Trade Union Council, 22nd Annual Report, 1916, p. 2.

[4] The International Congress of Women '99. Women in Industrial Life, p. 184.

[5] ibid., p. 186.

[6] Christabel Pankhurst, Unshackled, The Story of How We Won the Vote, 1959, p. 41.

[7] Eva Gore Booth, op. cit., p. 12.

[8] ibid.

[9] Dr. L. Bather, Manchester and Salford Trades Council from 1880 unpublished thesis in Manchester University Arts' Library (1956).

[10] Manchester and Salford Trades Council, Annual Report and Directory 1936-37, Mary Quaile, J. P..

Chapter 5

Gathering Strength, 1900-1914.

"It grows, it grows, are we the same,
The feeble band, the few?
Or what are these with eyes aflame,
And hands to deal and do?"

No Master,

William Morris
(Chants of Labour No. 17).

The recurring problem of unemployment was
often discussed by the Trades Council. As early
as 1892, an approach was made to the local
authorities in Manchester and Salford asking for
public work to be provided for the unemployed.
In 1895, the Council organised an Emergency
Relief Fund. After the turn of the century, the
numbers of unemployed rose considerably. By
1903, the Council reported, "the scarcity of
employment has been keenly felt by many during
the past winter... Many of the destitute
unemployed are unskilled labourers, but we have
reason to believe that distress has been felt among
many who come under the heading of skilled
workers."[1]

In 1904, the Council sent a resolution to the
Lord Mayor of Manchester and the Mayor of
Salford. It called the attention of both Corporations
to "the deplorable facts that widespread destitution
and misery are rampant in our midst, owing to want
of employment, and that as a result hundreds of
men, women and children are lacking the bare
necessaries of life; the consequence being inevitable

loss of moral, mental and physical stamina."
They asked that "useful public work of a
serviceable character, at a fair rate of wages"
should be provided "with the least possible delay."[2]

The following year, the position had
deteriorated to such an extent that the unemployed
revolted. "Scenes occurred in Manchester this
afternoon which have no parallel in the history of
the city since the dreadful days of Peterloo nearly
a century ago."[3]   reported the Evening Chronicle
on 31st July. Meetings were held frequently in
Police Yard, Albert Street, in support of the
Unemployed Bill which was before the House of
Commons. This Bill, while totally inadequate, did
place some responsibility on the Government for
dealing with the problem in terms of creating work
of a national character. On 31st July, unemployed
workers met at one o'clock and were addressed by
Mr. Smith, Chairman of the Unemployed Committee,
W.E. Skevington, an active member of the S.D.F.,
and Mr. Greerson of Owen's College. Mr. McGregor
an unemployed worker from Salford, also spoke.
Smith said that unemployed workers must be
"prepared to fight to the death to push forward the
Bill."[4]   Other speakers condemned the attitude of
the Government and the inaction of the local
authorities. At the end of the meeting it was
announced that there would be a march to Piccadilly
to hold a further meeting. Smith and Skevington
marched at the head holding a banner inscribed,
"We demand the Unemployed Bill". The authorities
apparently lost their heads and drafted in a hundred
Police, who were available at the Town Hall. At
two-thirty, Cross Street was impassable. The
marchers shouted to stockbrokers as they passed
the Royal Exchange, "It's work we want". In

Market Street, the Police moved into action.
Batons were drawn and one inspector "broke his
thick stick on the head of one man." Another
man was "badly cut on the head and blood was
flowing freely down his face as he was taken to
the Royal Infirmary. Women screamed and men
stood in amazement."[5]   Messrs. Skevington,
McGregor and Steadman were arrested and taken
into the Town Hall. An editorial comment in the
press on the following day admitted, "Possibly
there was loss of temper and somewhat too ready
use of force."[6]

On the day after this display of Police brutality,
the unemployed rallied in force. A conference was
held between the Lord Mayor and the leaders of the
unemployed workers, at which the right to hold
meetings in Albert Square was conceded.

In 1908, with Labour a growing force on the
City Council, Concillor Tom Fox, the Secretary of
the Trades Council, moved a successful resolution
that £50,000 be borrowed to finance work for the
unemployed.

A 'Right To Work' Committee was set up by
the Trades Council in 1909. At a conference held
in Caxton Hall which was attended by two hundred
delegates, Alf Purcell, member of the Executive
Committee, moved a resolution calling for
insurance against unemployment. This declared
that any such scheme which might be in competition
with trade union unemployment funds should be
opposed and that the state should "guarantee
subsidies to bona fide trade unionists making
payment to their unemployed members."[7]
Charles Keen, the Vice-President of the Council,
moved that the school leaving age should become a
nationally enforced fourteen years and that the half-

time system should be abolished. In an omnibus resolution he also called for the compulsory feeding of necessitous children and a national system of children's employment committees.

After the Taff Vale Judgement in 1901, when the Council discussed the decision which awarded damages and costs to the Taff Vale Railway Company against the Amalgamated Society of Railway Servants for their action in striking and preventing the use of blackleg labour, the Secretary reported, "the highest Court of Appeal has decided that a trade union is a corporation capable of sueing and being sued, which is certainly a capital victory for capital at the expense of industry."[8] The effect of the judgement was to remove at a stroke the rights that unions had acquired under the Acts of 1871 and 1876. It made strikes virtually illegal. A campaign was started to change the law and establish protection for the unions. Trade unionists were compelled to face the fact that they could no longer be non-political.

The 1902 May Day demonstration went to Gorton Park, and three resolutions were adopted. The first called for every support to be given to efforts being made in the House of Commons to define the legal status of trade unions. The second demanded a non-contributory state pension scheme to enable all citizens, male and female, to retire at sixty. The last impressed on the local authorities of Manchester and Salford the necessity of borrowing money to purchase land and build cottages or tenements. The Councils already possessed the power under the Working Classes Act of 1890 to borrow money for an extended period and, as the resolution pointed out they would enjoy the ownership of the property when built.

This vexed problem of housing engaged the attention of the Council and in 1903, figures were published showing that in Manchester there were 34,147 people living in overcrowded houses. This was over six per cent of the population. In Salford, the situation was even worse, with 16,653 needing rehousing, a seven and a half per cent figure. The Trades Council again spotlighted this social evil in 1904, when it pressed its case on the local Governing Board in a resolution, "to secure that all new housing areas shall be planned to ensure an ample provision of light and air." This, they said, would render impossible, "the development of new slums."[9] They also called for effective powers to deal with the housing question in rural areas.

The Council kept up the agitation arising out of Taff Vale and gave support to the Trades Union and Trades Dispute Bill which, by 1904, had passed its second reading in the House of Commons with a substantial majority. The Council pledged itself not to give support to any candidate who failed "to declare his intention to vote for the Bill."[10]

In 1906, G.D. Kelley resigned as Secretary to the Council on being elected as Member of Parliament. He was among the first Labour M.P.s. His successor was Tom Fox.

Tom Fox was born in Stalybridge on 21st December, 1860. He went to work as a half-timer in a cotton mill at a very early age and then left the mill to work in a shop. When he was twenty-one, he joined the Liverpool Regiment and served eight years in India and Burma. He reached the rank of Sergeant. When he returned to civilian life, he worked as a labourer in a foundry for eighteen shillings a week, and later he became a boilermaker's labourer. His interest in the labour movement arose

from reading Blatchford's articles in the Sunday Chronicle, and in 1890 he became associated with Leonard Hall in organising labourers in the Lancashire and Adjoining Counties Labour Amalgamation. Fox rapidly became a member of the Executive Committee, and Secretary of the Dukinfield Branch. When Hall resigned the General Secretaryship, Fox was elected to the position. He joined the I.L.P. from its inception and in 1904 was elected to Manchester City Council as Labour membe for Bradford Ward. Colleagues described him as, "A hard hitter, a clean fighter, a worthy antagonist and a staunch friend."[11] He was a "forceful speake and efficient Chairman." His "burly figure, button tight in his reefer jacket" was "familiar to trade unionists of the North as a trusted leader."[12]
After three years, Tom Fox resigned from the Secretaryship of the Trades Council and William Mellor was elected in his place.

Unlike Tom Fox, Mellor was a Mancunian born and bred. His home was in Clock Alley, a street absorbed by the Co-operative Wholesale Society's premises off Corporation Street. Although he attended the Cathedral School, he had to leave early to go to work at the age of ten. He left, however, with a taste for reading which remained with him for life. He joined the Bennett Street Sunday School and attended George Milner's English Literature Class. Under such devoted guidance, he developed his literary taste. He also joined the Literary Society, where he practised public speaking and acquired the facility to write fluent English. He passed through the courses on History, Literature and Economics, and then returned to his old school as a tutor, a position he retained for much of his life. The Recreational Lectures held at the Ancoats Brotherhoo attracted his interest and, arising from his attendance there, he won an extension scholarship to Oxford. He followed the trade of bookbinder, and became active in the National Union of Bookbinders and Machine Rulers. He held almost every local office and became editor of the Bookbinding Trades Journal. Politically, he joined the Independent Labour Party and was a foundation member of the Manchester Labour Representation Committee. He was described by one of his colleagues as having a "kind disposition, human feeling and a strong sense of justice." He was also characterised as, "quiet, unostentatious, almost reserved."[13]

On 16th March, 1910, the Council affiliated to the Workers' Educational Association and urged its associated branches to do the same. The W.E.A. was described as, "Unsectarian, non-party and democratic."[14] Full support was given to a meeting in the Free Trade Hall on 20th October, where the speakers included Professor Sadler, Bishop of Birmingham, J.R. Clynes, M.P., and Miss Margaret McMillan.

In that year the Council adopted the group system of organisation. Each Union was allocated to a group based on an industry such as building, engineering and printing. Delegates attended group meetings monthly as well as the regular Council meetings. Two members from each group were elected to the Executive Committee.

Ernest Jones Memorial

In 1913, the Trades Union Congress was held in Manchester. While it was in session, the Trades Council took advantage of the occasion to pay tribute to the work of Ernest Jones, the Chartist. The

65

memorial stone on the grave in Ardwick Cemetery was restored and re-engraved by the Council. On Sunday afternoon, August 31st, T.U.C. delegates and Manchester trades unionists were invited to attend the ceremony at the Cemetery. Councillor Tom Fox presided and said that they were "met to do homage to a hero who, in days when it was a dangerous and difficult thing to voice the rights of the common people, had not feared to go wherever duty pointed... He had preached the gospel of justice to the common people, had suffered long imprisonment, and they for whom he had suffered would be cravens indeed if they permitted his memorial to be forgotten." He said that the restoration was "a mark of their esteem for a man who was a poet, an orator, and, above all, essentially a good man."[15] The memorial was then unveiled by Mr. W.J. Davis, the President of the Trades Union Congress. He thanked the Trades Council for having given them the opportunity of honouring the memory of a great champion of the people

International Affairs

In 1900, when the country was involved in fighting the Boers in South Africa, the Council declared that any settlement must protect the rights of labour. Three years later, it helped to organise a demonstration against the Russian Tsarist Government to protest against its anti Jewish pogroms. In 1904, the South African situation again demanded the attention of British trade unionists and the Council supported agitation against the importation of Chinese labour into South Africa.

In 1905, the Council listened to an address by the Hon. Mr. Gopal Krishna Gokhale, Congress delegate from the province of Bombay. Mr. Gokhale convinced delegates of the justice of the Indian people's case which he had been entrusted to put to the people of this country and they passed a resolution to be sent to the Prime Minister, the Secretary of State for India and the Leader of the Opposition in the House of Commons, saying that they were of the opinion that "the people should have a fair share in the management of Indian affairs." [16]

The situation in Russia, where the Czar ruled with despotic power, was noted with growing alarm. Pogroms of Jews and other minorities, and severe restrictions on the lives of all ordinary people led the Council to express "horror and indignation" when the Czar visited England in 1909.

By 1912, the international situation had developed to a stage where the very real danger of war breaking out could be clearly seen. The Council discussed this danger and gave unanimous support to the resolution of the British Bureau of the Labour and Socialist International. This called on "organised working class movement of all countries... to come to a mutual agreement whereby in the event of war being threatened between any two or more countries, the workers of those countries would hold themselves prepared to try to prevent it by mutual and simultaneous stoppage of work in the countries affected." [17]

South Africa again occupied the attention of the Council in 1913 when they protested against the use of British troops on the Rand. They expressed solidarity with the South African miners who were trying to obtain human conditions. The following year, before the outbreak of war, the Council organised a meeting on March 8th at the Free Trade Hall to protest against the deportation of South

African trade unionists. Together with the
Lancashire and Cheshire Federation of Trades
Councils, they sent ten pounds to the Trade Union
Congress Defence Fund.

Labour Representation
　　Before the turn of the century, the labour
movement had relied almost entirely on the dubious
support of the Liberal Party to take its case to
Parliament. By 1900, the need for direct
representation of labour had become urgent and trade
unions began to take more energetic steps to increase
Labour representation both in the House of Commons
and on Municipal bodies.
　　G.D. Kelley, Secretary of the Trades Council,
was present at the foundation conference of the
Labour Representation Committee held in the Memorial
Hall, London, in February, 1900. He attended as a
delegate from the Lithographic Printers. On his
return, he reported to the Council and they decided to
affiliate to the L.R.C. They were one of the seven
out of a total of one hundred and seventy-one trades
councils who decided to take this important step. As
an indication of the need that they felt for direct
representation, they offered hospitality to the L.R.C.
for their next conference and arranged to do the
necessary organisational work. The first Annual
Conference was therefore held in Manchester at the
Co-operative Hall, Downing Street, in February, 1901.
Among the Manchester delegates were, F.Entwistle
and G.D. Kelley from the Trades Council, and Tom
Fox and Matthew Arrandale from their own Societies.
　　The following year, early in 1902, the Council
called a Conference at which the Manchester and
Salford Representation Committee was formed. John
Edward Sutton, a forty year old miner, was elected

as Secretary. He had begun work down the pit when he was seven and a half. As early as 1894, he had been elected to the Manchester City Council and had served twenty years as Secretary to the Bradford Miners. He was Checkweighman at Bradford Colliery for twenty-six years and only resigned when he was elected as Member of Parliament for East Manchester in 1910.

G.D. Kelley announced in 1904 that he had finally broken with the Liberal Party. However, the Liberals made their own assessment of Kelley and continued to give him full support.

A further step was taken in 1905 when the Trades Council called a Conference to discuss local Labour Representation. A resolution was passed calling on all affiliated Societies to contribute a sum of not less than one penny per member for the purpose of assisting in the election of Labour candidates. This fund was to be disbursed by the Executive Committee of the Council to those candidates who were prepared to sign a pledge similar to that insisted upon by the National L.R.C.. Furthermore, they had to be "members of a bona-fide trade union, the Independent Labour Party or Social Democratic Federation."[18]

It is significant that both the I.L.P. and the S.D.F. were offered support in this resolution. The part played by the S.D.F. can perhaps be best illustrated by the work of one of its most active members, George Tabbron. In 1889, he was active with Bill Horrocks and George Evans in organising the Gas workers. He was a craftsman and member of the Manchester Brassfounders and Finishers' Society. It is possible that he was a delegate to the Council in the eighties because he was elected to the Executive Committee in 1893 and in 1898 he became

Vice-President. He was President of the Council from 1899 to 1901 and in 1905 he was a delegate from the Council to the Annual Conference of the Labour Representation Committee.

The Trades Council continued to maintain a close relationship with the Manchester L.R.C.. In 1906, three men sat on the Executive Committee of both bodies; in 1907, there were six, in 1908, two, and in 1909, one. Although the Trades Council affiliated to the L.R.C. at National level in 1901, the Manchester Committee did not do so until 1913.

The Liberal victory of 1906, when twenty-nine Labour Members were elected, led workers to believe that something would be done to improve wages and conditions. The reverse took place. Real wages dropped from 100 in 1900 to 92 in 1911. Dissatisfaction with the Parliamentary Labour Party began to develop within the trades union movement and workers turned to industrial action to defend their wages and conditions. When Tom Mann returned to England in 1910 from a visit to South Africa, the industrial barometer had already moved to stormy and the decline in real wages was leading to a revolt on the part of the working class.

Mann launched a campaign advocating higher wages, improved working conditions, an end to craft sectionalism and stronger unity and organisation on a class basis. In order to further these objectives, a conference was held at the Coal Exchange in Manchester on November 26th, 1910, at which the Trades Council was represented by R. Lundy of the National Society of Operative Printers' Assistants and D. Machin of the Braziers and Sheet Metal Workers' Union. In the Chair was Alf Purcell, Organiser of the National Furnishing Trades Association and a long standing member of the Social

Democratic Federation (re-named the British Socialist Party).

Purcell was a man of great physical vigour with an imposing personality. He was also an impressive orator. Well known as an ardent Socialist, he was often found at Hyndman Hall in Liverpool Street, Salford. He had been a delegate to the Trades Council from 1902 and occupied the Presidential Chair in 1905/6 and again in 1914 to 1919, during the war years. He served on the Executive Committee from 1910 to 1922. He became a Member of Parliament and played a prominent part in the trade union movement at National and International level and then returned to Manchester to take over the Secretaryship of the Trades Council in 1929.

At the 1910 Conference he struck the note that "the thing needed to emancipate the workers as a class" is not to federate but "to amalgamate their movement to such an extent that whenever one worker was attacked - be he joiner, plasterer, labourer, shop assistant, tiler, or even the man who, in the future, would probably be called on to drive an airship - any attack upon any one worker would be the signal for the resentment of the whole of the workers throughout the industrial world."[19] These principles were those advocated by the industrial syndicalists and after the Conference, Tom Mann was invited by Manchester Trades Council to address a meeting on industrial unionism.

This meeting took place at the Memorial Hall in Albert Square on December 7th, 1910. Tom Mann was described as a "human dynamo". He spoke with terrific rapidity, yet every word was as clear as a bell... he swept over crowds like a whirlwind; his

mastery of the art of oratory was superb."[20]
At the meeting he defined industrial unionism as
taking "such action as to enable the workers to be
the decisive factor" in determining "how they
should manipulate the tools of production."[21]   He
advocated organisation of the unskilled, mass
action and the unity of all trade unions.

The seamen and dockers were the first to
demonstrate that militant industrial action could
compel the employers to make substantial
concessions. The Liverpool Transport workers'
strike in 1911 was led by Tom Mann and it proved
to be an object lesson to the whole trade union
movement. The railway workers took up the
cudgels with the first national railway strike
involving fifty thousand men, both those in the union
and those as yet unorganised. The strike was spread
by the rank and file throughout the country. On the
Lancashire and Cheshire Railway, the strike began
in Liverpool and by August 18th had spread to
Manchester. The Manchester Guardian lamented
that "The strike, yesterday, disorganised or stopped
the Manchester traffic to such an extent and in such
a manner"[22] that it was unprecedented. Central
Station was closed. All goods traffic was stopped.
Pickets stood listlessly at the stations with no duties
to perform.

The significance of these events was indicated
at a meeting organised by the Trades Council on
October 8th, 1911 at the Grand Theatre. Charles
Kean, President of the Council, was in the Chair and
he read out letters of support that had been received
from Ben Tillett, Councillor Tom Fox and H.
Jachade, Secretary of the International Transport
Workers' Federation. The resolution moved by
Councillor Titt was seconded by Sarah Dickenson,

DEAR SIR,

You are hereby informed that the ORDINARY MONTHLY MEETING of the Council will be held on **Wednesday, May 17th, 1911,** at the **CAXTON HALL, Chapel Street, Salford,** at **8-0** prompt.

The following business will be brought before the Meeting :—

1.—Minutes of last Meeting.

2.—Minutes of E.C.

3.—Correspondence.

4.—RESOLUTIONS :—

" That this Council, representing thirty thousand organised workers, whilst welcoming the introduction of "The Shops Bill," further calls upon the Government to include the following Amendments :

1st.—A sixty hours week including meal times of adequate length, not less than one hour for dinner and half-an-hour for tea.

2nd.—Compulsory closing of all Shops with a statutory Half Holiday.

3rd.—That the term Shop Assistants includes any person employed in or about a retail establishment not affected by the Factory Acts.

Further that it is imperative in the clause relating to closing orders the word "shall" be inserted in place of "may." This we consider necessary for the purpose of making the Bill effective, and reducing the difficulties of inspection. Copies of this resolution to be sent to the Prime Minister, Home Secretary and Local M.P.'s."

Distributive Trades Group.

Secretary of the Women's Trades and Labour Council. It read, "This mass meeting of workers while viewing with satisfaction the recent advances made by organised labour, desires to emphasise the absolute necessity for more general and effective organisation in the future in order to secure still further betterment of working conditions for both men and women."[23]   After Alf Purcell had spoken, J. McGlasson moved a further resolution condemning the Home Secretary, Mr. Winston Churchill, for sending troops to Manchester during the rail strike. This was, he said, "in complete disregard of the wishes of the Lord Mayor and the Watch Committee." The military had been sent, "not to protect property, but to intimidate the men who were involved in an industrial dispute."[24].

In his Report to the Council for 1911, William Mellor drew the lesson of these stirring events. He said, "1911 did not simply make a record, it ushered in a new era in industrial conflicts. For the first time in England, the 'sympathetic strike' was evoked on a large scale and effectively used as a weapon of industrial warfare." One notable feature of the labour advance is that it was mainly confined to the least well organised and poorest paid workers. Mellor pointed out that there had been "an immense increase of membership in many of the unions engaged in this industrial crusade." He said moreover that Manchester had "led and set the pace in the Transport Workers' Movement, and other large centres followed quickly." The railway strike in August, he pointed out, was "a movement that brought home to the nation in most dramatic fashion the complete dependence of the community on an unregarded section of the workers for the bare necessities of life." He rammed home the lesson that "never before was the nation so nearly face to face with a food famine as it was during the railway strike of 1911. "[25]

The Don't Shoot Leaflet

Following the use of troops in industrial disputes, a Liverpool stonemason, Fred Bowers, wrote an appeal to the soldiers which has become known as the "Don't Shoot Leaflet". This was first published in the 'Irish Worker' and then circulated by a railwayman, Fred Crowley, as a leaflet among the men stationed at Aldershot. Tom Mann reprinted it in his paper 'The Syndicalist' of January, 1912.

On 14th March, he quoted from the appeal at a meeting in Salford Town Hall where he was speaking to a meeting of the Workers' Union, of which he was Vice-President. He was subsequently charged with incitement to mutiny and at Manchester Assize Court on 9th May, he was sentenced to three months' imprisonment.

This proved to be a rallying point for the whole labour movement. The Trades Council set up a Defence Fund and a series of meetings and protests was organised. In seven weeks, Tom Mann was released and he wrote, it was due "to the many meetings held and resolutions carried." He also commented that credit was due for "sending them to the right quarter, plus the determination to take further action if necessary. "[26]   The Trades Council, by its organisation was able to coordinate and centralise activity generated by wide sections of the labour movement.

The climax to this stormy period was the Dublin lock out of 1913. This was described as "the highest point reached in the class struggle in Europe in the period leading up to the 1914 war. "[27]

HALT ! ATTENTION ! !

Open Letter to British Soldiers.

This letter to British soldiers, reprinted from *Sheldrake's Military Gazette* (Aldershot), of March 1st, 1912, is the subject of the charge against Crowsley, Guy Bowman, the Buck brothers, and Tom Mann. Read and judge for yourself. Let the voice of the PEOPLE be heard.

Men ! Comrades ! Brothers !

You are in the Army

So are WE. YOU in the Army of Destruction. We in the Industrial, or Army of Construction.

WE work at mine, mill, forge, factory, or dock, producing and transporting all the goods, clothing, stuffs, etc., which make it possible for people to live.

YOU ARE WORKING MEN'S SONS.

When WE go on Strike to better OUR lot, which is the lot also of YOUR FATHERS, MOTHERS, BROTHERS, and SISTERS, YOU are called upon by your officers to MURDER US.

DON'T DO IT !

You know how it happens always has happened.

We stand out as long as we can. Then one of our (and your) irresponsible Brothers, goaded by the sight and thought of his and his loved ones' misery and hunger, commits a crime on property. Immediately You are ordered to MURDER Us, as You did at Mitchelstown, at Featherstone, at Belfast.

Don't You know that when You are out of the colours. and become a "Civy" again, that You, like Us, may be on Strike, and You, like Us, be liable to be MURDERED by other soldiers.

BOYS, DON'T DO IT !

"THOU SHALT NOT KILL," says the Book.

DON'T FORGET THAT !

It does not say, "unless you have a uniform on."

No ! MURDER IS MURDER, whether committed in the heat of anger on one who has wronged a loved one, or by pipe-clayed Tommies with a rifle.

BOYS, DON'T DO IT !

ACT THE MAN ! ACT THE BROTHER ACT THE HUMAN BEING !

Property can be replaced ! Human life, never.

The Idle Rich Class, who own and order you about, own and order us about also. They and their friends own the land and means of life of Britain.

YOU DON'T. WE DON'T.

When WE kick, they order YOU to MURDER Us.

When You kick, You get courtmartialed and cells.

YOUR fight is OUR fight. Instead of fighting AGAINST each other, WE should be fighting with each other.

Out of OUR loins, OUR lives, OUR homes, You came.

Don't disgrace YOUR PARENTS, YOUR CLASS, by being the willing tools any longer of the MASTER CLASS.

YOU, like Us, are of the SLAVE CLASS. WHEN WE rise, YOU rise ; when WE fall, even by your bullets, YE fall also.

England with its fertile valleys and dells, its mineral resources, its sea harvests, is the heritage of ages to us.

YOU no doubt joined the Army out of poverty.

WE work long hours for small wages at hard work, because of OUR poverty. And both YOUR poverty and OURS arises from the fact that Britain with its resources belongs to only a few people. These few, owning Britain, own OUR jobs. Owning OUR jobs, they own OUR very LIVES.

Comrades, have WE called in vain ? Think things out and refuse any longer to MURDER YOUR KINDRED. Help Us to win back BRITAIN for the BRITISH, and the WORLD for the WORKERS.

Eighty thousand workers led by James Larkin and James Connolly defied intimidation and police terror aimed to smash the Irish Transport and General Workers' Union. Two strikers were killed and four hundred wounded. British workers gave strong support to the Dublin strikers. A series of food ships sailed from Manchester to Dublin loaded with food supplied by the Cooperative Wholesale Society and paid for with money collected by the trades union movement.

The Trades Council worked hard for the cause. At a mass meeting held in Alexandra Park on Sunday, September 14th, 1913, Tom Fox, President of the Council, took the Chair and the President of the Dublin District Committee of the Amalgamated Society of Engineers and a member of the Dublin City Council, Brother Partridge, made the main speech. He cited the case of a girl who received 10d (approx 4p) for a week's work in a factory. He showed a broken truncheon which, he said, had been shattered on the head of an unoffending citizen, adding grimly that the owner would not need it for some time. Alf Purcell moved the resolution, seconded by C. Kean, "That this meeting records its emphatic condemnation of the brutal interference with the rights of the citizens of Dublin in prohibiting the holding of a public meeting in O'Connell Street. We further call upon the Chief Constable to instigate a rigid inquiry into the outrages committed by the Police, with a view to finding out who is responsible for the murder of two people and inflicting severe injuries upon hundreds of other unoffending citizens."[28]

The Trades Council raised £472 and sent seventeen bales of clothing to Dublin via the C.W.S.. Important as such aid was, it was inadequate to meet the needs of the situation. The British trade union movement needed to organise a strike in sympathy with the Irish workers, but this action was not taken and the locked out men were eventually forced back to work by starvation.

These stirring years, 1910 to 1914, are often called 'The Great Unrest'. They were years of growth and consolidation so far as the Manchester and Salford Trades Council was concerned. During the four war years, working class activity did not cease, but it took different forms. The Trades Council played its full part then as it had in those formative years up to 1914.

References

[1] Manchester and Salford Trades and Labour Council Annual Report, 1903.

[2] ibid., 1904.

[3] Manchester Evening Chronicle, 31st July, 1905.

[4] ibid.

[5] ibid.

[6] ibid., 1st August, 1905.

[7] Manchester and Salford Trades and Labour Council Annual Report, 1910.

[8] ibid., 1902.

[9] ibid., 1904.

[10] ibid.

[11] Trades Union Congress Official Souvenir Manchester 1913.

[12] Manchester Guardian, 3rd March, 1934.

[13] T.U.C. Souvenir 1913, op. cit.

[14] Manchester and Salford Trades and Labour Council Annual Report, 1910.

[15] ibid., 1913.

[16] ibid., 1905

[17] Press cutting - scrap book - source unknown - authors' possession.

[18] Manchester and Salford Trades and Labour Council Annual Report, 1905.

[19] Industrial Syndicalist, December, 1910.

[20] Bonar Thompson, Hyde Park Orator, 1934, p. 88.

[21] Manchester Guardian, 8th December, 1910.

[22] ibid., 19th August, 1911.

[23] ibid., 9th October, 1911.

[24] ibid.

[25] Manchester and Salford Trades and Labour Council Annual Report, 1911.

[26] Tom Mann Memoirs, 1923, pp. 313-4.

[27] Desmond Greaves, James Connolly, The Life and Times, 1961.

[28] Manchester Guardian, 15th September, 1913.

" LEST WE FORGET "

THE GREAT WAR.

The primary object of this war and of all wars is to lacerate human flesh, to break bones, to inflict torture, to paralyse and to kill. Every army in the field to-day is out for maiming and homicide, and for nothing else. Certainly armies make prisoners, but not because they want to do so, rather because they are afraid to carry out logically their principles. Every explosive weapon, from the 42-centimetre gun to the service revolver, is designed, made, charged, and fired with the definite and clear intention of either doing men to death or inflicting upon them the severest possible disablement, which must nearly always be accompanied by intense physical pain, and which very often involves lifelong misery and woe. Guns are aimed against buildings only for the reason that they serve, directly or indirectly, to protect men from murder and disablement, and the purpose of destroying buildings is to deprive men of some kind of defence, and thus expose them to destruction, torture, and paralysis. This is war. This is the confessed first aim of Prussia and all militarists, for no ulterior military aim can be achieved until this aim is achieved. This is what is going on daily just now in many different parts of Europe, against the outraged conscience of the world. This is the basis of military glory and of all those other fustian things that overlords rant about. This is what overlords wish to perpetuate among the usages of mankind. Let us never forget that war is first and last the tearing of human flesh, the shattering of human bones, and the greatest source of human agony, both physical and mental.—*Arnold Bennett,*

Chapter 6

The Council in Wartime, 1914-1918

"Stone-axe and club and brazen
                          sword
Have given place
To weapons of a less heroic mould -
More cruel, and more cunning, and
                          more base -
And murder's vast machinery
          dominates the world."

                          Europe 1916.
                          Bertram Lloyd.

The endorsement by the Council of the
Labour and Socialist International resolution to
oppose war by means of a general strike was not
put into effect. No preparations were made either
in Manchester or elsewhere to implement such a
policy. Certainly the Council's report for 1914
contained Arnold Bennett's description of the
horrors of war. But after August 1914, the trade
union and Labour leaders decided to give support
to the war and to enter into an industrial truce.
By May, 1915, leading Labour Members of
Parliament had agreed to serve in the War Cabinet.
    The Trades Council became involved in the
day to day problems arising from war profiteering
and rent racking. A Tenants' Defence Association
was set up as a sub-committee with William Mellor
as Secretary. Later, the Association became an
independent organisation although the Council
continued to assist with financial and legal help.
Eventually, the Government was forced to introduce

a Rent Restrictions Act.

The major industry in Manchester was engineering and this became a vital part of the war machine. The workers in engineering were confronted with a number of problems. They had to contend with the call-up, dilution (allowing women to undertake work traditionally reserved for men who had served an apprenticeship and paying them at a lower rate), and considerable changes in established workshop customs and practice. The centre of gravity moved from the trade union movement to the workshop floor, and there was a rapid growth of the Shop Stewards' Movement.

A Manchester Workers' Committee was formed by active shop stewards in April, 1916. In September, engineering workers were awarded three shillings a week increase for time workers. Most Manchester factories operated a piece work system and therefore did not qualify for the rise. This naturally created considerable indignation. On 22nd December, two thousand workers went on strike. The Executive Council of the Amalgamated Society of Engineers persuaded them to resume work, but the strike committee which had been set up remained in being and later merged with the Manchester Workers' Committee to form a Manchester Joint Engineering Shop Stewards' Committee. George Peet, an A.S.E. Branch Secretary and Shop Steward at Gorton Railway Works (Gorton Tank), was elected Secretary.

The spark which ignited the smouldering resentment in Manchester was a strike at Tweedale and Smalleys in Rochdale. They objected to the use of dilutees on work which was not directly connected with the war effort and which they called 'commercial work'. The Manchester Committee had been preparing for action and was ready. On 22nd April, 1917, a mass meeting was held and a resoltuon passed which registered a "vigorous protest against the proposed withdrawal of the trade exemption cards."[1] This issue arose alongside that of women replacing men on skilled work. Craftsmen were issued with exemption cards which excused them from military service. The Committee decided to take a ballot vote in the workshops to decide whether to take strike action. The favourable result of this ballot encouraged them to call a strike to begin at 5.30 p.m., on Monday, 30th April. The District Committee of the A.S.E. sent officials to discuss the situation with the shop stewards and George Peet was reported as having told them that "they had taken this action which had nothing to do with Societies. It was purely a rank and file movement taken unofficially and with full knowledge of their responsibilities." The Officials were told that they "were powerless to do anything in the matter."[2]

By 4th May, the strike had escalated and sixty thousand workers in eighteen Lancashire towns were involved. It continued to gain strength and soon there were a quarter of a million workers on strike in forty-eight towns. The shop stewards attempted direct negotiation with the Government, but at a conference at the Fellowship Hall in London, police raided the meeting and George Peet and Percy Keeley from Manchester with seven others were arrested. In spite of this, the strike remained solid in Manchester and the return to work was only effected after most other districts.

The Government was forced to make concessions. The arrested men were released on an undertaking to support a call for a return to work. The result of this action was that the Shop Stewards' Movement gained recognition as a powerful force in the workshops and its work was reflected in the Trades Council after the war was over. Jack Munro, one of the leaders of the Manchester Engineering Joint Shop Stewards' Committee became President and, later, Secretary of the Trades Council.

The Revolution in Russia in 1917 had an immediate impact on the British labour movement. William Mellor wrote, "While despotism remains there can be no permanent peace. When they have been deposed, as Russia has so gloriously deposed its hated oligarchy, Labour will desire no conquests, and no national exterminations."[3]   Under the influence of the Revolution, a Convention was held in Leeds on 3rd June, 1917, with over a thousand delegates. It was decided to set up a Council of Workers' and Soldiers' delegates. Although there is no evidence that the Trades Council sent representatives to this Convention, they did elect two delegates to a subsequent Divisional Conference held in Manchester. Because no hall could be hired for the conference, it was actually held in Southport. It had little influence on events.

Towards the end of 1917, the shortage of food became acute. Paisley District Committee of the A.S.E. wrote to the Manchester Committee drawing their attention to the rise in the cost of living which had shot up by over one hundred per cent. They commented that the Government had failed to regulate wages to keep pace with this inflation. The District Committee were "in full sympathy with the points raised" and were "prepared to take any action necessary to obtain the objects desired." They wrote both to Lord Rhonda, the Food Controller and

Manchester and Salford Trades Council "respecting the difficulties, inconveniences, and the degradation our wives have to undergo in order to obtain the mere necessities of life."[4]

On January 14th, 1918, the A.S.E. District Committee called on all its members to "cease work on Saturday morning at 9 a.m., then march in procession from their respective workshops to demonstrate and protest against the present unequal distribution of food, and that the Trades Councils of Manchester and Gorton be informed of our intentions and they be asked to cooperate with us."[5] This they did, for a united working class demonstration took place. The march converged on Albert Square where Alf Purcell, President of the Trades Council, led a deputation to meet the Lord Mayor. Other members of the delegation included William Mellor, Secretary of the Trades Council, the Vice-President, R.J. Davies, who also represented Manchester Labour Party, T.I. Holt, District Secretary of the A.S.E., Jack Munro and A. Leacy of the Manchester Joint Engineering Shop Stewards' Committee together with Councillors Hague and Binns. A Manifesto approved by the demonstrators concluded, "Don't mock us with expressions of sympathy... insist that from the absolute source of supply to the actual places of distribution that it shall not only be adequately controlled but that it shall be equally distributed."[6]

The Trades Council emerged from the war with an increased affiliated membership and strengthened organisation. The position of Secretary had been made full time and an office in Clarence Street, off Albert Square in the City centre had been opened. The absorption of the two Womens' Councils again increased the number of delegates. These preparations stood the Council in good stead when the sharp class battles that loomed on the horizon at the end of the war became immediate and urgent reality.

References

[1] Manchester District Committee Amalgamated Society of Engineers Minutes, 1st May, 1917.

[2] ibid., 4th May, 1917

[3] Manchester and Salford Trades and Labour Council Annual Report, 1917.

[4] Manchester District Committee Amalgamated Society of Engineers Minutes, 27th November, 1917.

[5] ibid., 11th January, 1918.

[6] Manchester Guardian, 28th January, 1918.

Chapter 7

Labour Aroused, 1919-1929.

"But we are the people of England; and we have
not spoken yet.
Smile at us, pay us, pass us. But do not quite
forget."

The Secret People,
G. K. Chesterton.

The success of the October Revolution in
Russia filled the British Government with fear.
They felt it necessary to send troops to try to
restore the status quo and prevent the spread of
disaffection to England. As early as January,
1919, the Council adopted a resolution calling for
the withdrawal of British troops from Russia.
On 2nd February, a "Hands Off Russia"
demonstration was held at the Free Trade Hall.
The object was "to protest against Allied
intervention and to demand the withdrawal of
Allied troops from Russia."[1]   The organisers
of this rallying call were the Manchester and
District United Socialist Council. The constituent
parts of the Council were the British Socialist
Party, the Socialist Labour Party and the
Independent Labour Party. Their representatives
were the chief speakers, John McLean, William
Paul and Jack Murphy.
Manchester was kept informed of
developments in Russia through the sympathetic
reports written by M. Philips Price in the
Manchester Guardian. Many trade unionists
preferred to keep themselves up to date by reading
these reports rather than the lies, hatred and

slander which appeared in the gutter press. They also had the penny pamphlets issued by the People's Russian Information Bureau. One of these reprinted Lenin and Tititcherine's appeal to the British troops in Russia, "Are You A Trade Unionist?".

A national "Hands Off Russia" Committee was established at the Socialist Hall in Openshaw. Alf Purcell was the President. This Committee linked the many local groups which preceded it. The Manchester and District Committee organised another Free Trade Hall meeting on 21st June. Robert Smillie, President of the Miners' Federation of Great Britain, and Robert Williams of the National Amalgamated Labourers' Union of Great Britain and Ireland were the chief speakers, and J. Brassington, the District Organiser of the National Union of Railwaymen was in the Chair. The views of the Trades Council were expressed by its Vice-President, Councillor Rhys Davies. Born in Carmarthenshire in 1877, the son of a roadmender, Davies began work at a very early age as a farm labourer. Three years later he became a collier and worked for the next ten years in the pit, striving to build up the South Wales Miners' Federation. During the strike in 1898, he organised a choir of thirty miners who toured England and Wales raising funds in aid of the striking colliers. He left the mines to work as a cashier for a Cooperative Society and in 1912 became a full-time officer of the Amalgamated Union of Cooperative Employees. By this time he had moved to Manchester, and in 1913 he was elected to Manchester City Council. Later he became a Member of Parliament. He was described as "an incisive and sometimes eloquent speaker and writer on industrial and economic subjects, a singer of no mean merit, and above and beyond all, a mercurial Welshman of abounding vitality and enthusiasm."[2]

Influential in both the industrial and political wings of the labour movement, Davies moved the composite resolution on Allied Intervention in Russia at the Labour Party Conference on 27th June, 1919. This called for the "Immediate cessation of intervention" and instructed the National Executive "to consult the Parliamentary Committee of the Trade Union Congress, with a view to effective action being taken to enforce these demands by the unreserved use of their political and industrial power." Rhys Davies concluded his supporting speech by saying, "If the Allies defeat the working class of Russia, they defeat the working class of this country." He also emphasised that "he had still to learn that because a movement was unconstitutional, it was wrong."[3] The resolution was adopted.

On April 30th, 1920, the Daily Herald alerted the movement to fresh dangers. "New Try To Crush Russia" said the headline. Polish armies with the full support of the Allies had launched an attack on a two hundred and fifty mile front. British trade unionists sprang to the defence of the first Workers' Republic. On 10th May, 1920, the London Dockers refused to load munitions on the Jolly George, destined for Poland. This gave impetus to the Hands Off Russia campaign.

By August, the Red Army had retaliated and launched a brilliant counter offensive while Europe seethed in a state of revolutionary ferment. This intensified the danger of Allied intervention. On Wednesday, 4th August, the British Government sent a threatening note to Russia and the movement against intervention gained added impetus. In Manchester, a united protest movement had built up by the weekend. That Saturday, August 7th,

Councillor William Mellor, Secretary of the Trades Council, sent a telegram to the Prime Minister protesting against the Government's "menacing and provocative attitude."[4]

On Sunday, August 8th, a Citizens' demonstration was held and on the following Monday a joint conference of the leaders of the Trades Union Congress, Labour Party and Parliamentary Labour Party was held in the House of Commons and a Council of Action was set up. In Manchester, the same evening, a meeting organised by the Trades Council and Labour Party was held in Stevenson's Square. Over five thousand were present and the chief speaker was Ellen Wilkinson. The Reverend J.J. Wilson, of St. Michael's in Angel Meadow, was also among the speakers. The audience cheered the denunciation of British intervention in Russia and booed vigorously when the name of Mr. Churchill, the Secretary for War, was mentioned. A resolution was adopted which stated "that this meeting of Manchester citizens of all shades of opinion and all creeds, protests in the strongest possible manner against any attempt on the part of the Government to intervene against Russia in the Russia-Polish situation either by the use of troops, the blockade, finance or the supply of munitions." The resolution went on to urge workers "to use every means in their power, both political and industrial, to defeat the purpose of the Government."[5]

The same week, the Trades Council received a telegram from the London Council of Action, of which Alf Purcell was one of the five members. It read, "Council of Action invites your Executive send representatives Special Conference, Central Hall, Westminster, Friday, 13th, 10. o'clock discuss Russian Polish war (with a view to) industrial action

prevent British intervention."[6]   Over a thousand
delegates met at the Special Conference. Although
there is no direct evidence, it is more than likely
that William Mellor would represent the Trades
Council. The Conference authorised the Council of
Action "to call for any and every withdrawal of
labour which circumstances may require."[7]
J.R. Clynes, the Member of Parliament for Miles
Platting, who represented the Parliamentary Labour
Party, emphasised that there had "been no wavering
of decision of any kind on the part of the whole of the
members of the Parliamentary Labour Party."[8]

The Manchester meetings continued. On the
10th, a further meeting was held in Stevenson's
Square. Coincidental with the Special Conference
on the 13th, Tom Louth of the National Union of
Railwaymen dealt with the right of railwaymen not to
carry munitions. He said they "were bound to take
such a stand some time and this appeared to be the
time."[9]   A Manchester Council of Action was set
up on August 15th at a joint meeting of the Manchester
Trades Council, Gorton Trades Council and
Manchester Central Labour Party. One of its
promoters said its object was "to prevent war and
the weapon it proposes to use is the General Strike."
He agreed that its objects were "purely political".
Labour, he said, had "determined the country must
not be thrown into a war with Russia at the whim of
the Government of the day."[10]

The same day, a demonstration was held in
Platt Fields Park with Tom Mann and Ben Tillett as
the speakers. Tillett was reported as saying that
"if the present Government forced a war on Russia,
he would do his best to promote a revolution." He
also said that "unless war was prevented, Europe
would be in a state of starvation."[11]

Manchester Council of Action had the full support of ex-service men and women and pacifist organisations. At a "Stop The War" meeting of ex-servicemen it was decided to seek an alliance with the Council of Action and the National Union of Ex-servicemen. One speaker, with four years service behind him, said that he and thousands like him could not go to war again.

Sunday, August 22nd, was designated "Peace Day" and Manchester Council of Action called upon "all men and women of goodwill" to demonstrate in Platt Fields or Crowcroft Park. Moreover, "All preachers, speakers, teachers and any other person who takes part in any sphere of public life" were urged to "prepare their minds for peace". The statement also said that a refusal on the part of the workers to "produce, transport and distribute" as a protest against war, was a "very mild action indeed in comparison with slaying and maiming thousands of youths..."[12]

The Peace Day meeting in Platt Fields heard Dr. Robert Dunstan, Labour candidate for the Rusholme Division of Manchester, emphasise that "united Labour" had stepped in to say that it was the people who would have to do the fighting and supply the cannon fodder and "no one", he declared, "shall declare war without the people's consent."[13] This pressure that was being exerted throughout the country prevented the Government from declaring war. It was a decisive defeat for the warmongers, who were led by Winston Churchill. William Mellor reported to the Trades Council that the Council of Action "had a considerable influence in putting an end to the imperialistic adventures of the Government in Poland."[14]

Alf Purcell, Herbert Skinner and Richard

Wallhead had meanwhile been in Russia for six weeks. They left on May 11th and on their return described the hardships that the Russian people were having to endure as the result of the Allied Blockade. They also described the efforts being made by the Soviets to tackle the economic and social problems of a vast country ravaged by war and with the inheritance of years of neglect during the Czarist regime. Alf Purcell was deeply influenced by what he saw in Russia and it was said of him that "Since his first visit in 1920, he became Russia's staunch and trusted friend." Jack Munro, who paid him the tribute, also said that "In the face of all opposition both inside and outside the movement, he worked vigorously for understanding and friendship and lived to see the fruition of many of the gigantic plans which had not even been thought of when he first set foot there."[15]

Manchester Labour College

Many changes took place in the Trades Council in the immediate post war years. One influence was the growing movement for Independent Working Class Education. The Council had been affiliated to the Workers' Education Association for a number of years but the broad education which was offered did not entirely meet the needs of political workers.

The Plebs League, based on Marxism, had been formed at Ruskin College, Oxford, in 1909. It arose out of a strike of the students in protest against the dismissal of their Principal, Dennis Hird. Among the strikers was Jack Owen, a Manchester engineering worker. Jack Owen became a Labour City Councillor and later joined the Communist Party. He was a well known reporter for the Daily Worker until he died in March, 1957.

The main result of the strike was the formation of a Central Labour College where students attended for a year and returned to their work far better equipped to deal with the basic economic problems of workshop life. They, in their turn, passed on their knowledge in local classes and the movement grew. On May 3rd, 1919, a Labour College to serve the Manchester area was opened at 32a Dale Street, near Piccadilly. A campaign was then mounted to obtain trade union support.

Members of the Trades Council had become dissatisfied with the education offered by the W. E. A. and when Jack Halstead, a member of the Newton Heath 3rd Branch of the Amalgamated Engineering Union addressed them in December, 1920, on the subject of Independent Working Class Education, they were prepared to give it serious consideration. The significance of the "Independence" was implicit in the motto of the Plebs League which actively supported the Labour Colleges. "I can promise to be candid, but not impartial" said the Plebs and by that they meant that education was either in the workers' interests or against them. The Labour College set up by workers to serve the interests of workers was unashamedly partial and the Council decided that this partiality was in their best interest. They decided to affiliate and send two representatives to serve on the Committee. By 1922, the Manchester Labour College had 145 affiliated Trade Union Branches with twenty-seven and a half thousand members all interested in working class emancipation.

The Plebs Magazine recorded this and commented that "a few energetic Plebs working in Manchester and Salford Trades Council got a resolution carried which promises greater moral and financial support for Manchester and District Labour College."[16]   These "energetic Plebs" were also highly influential in the Council. Jack Munro was a Pleb and a class tutor. The Vice-President, J.B. Walker of the Amalgamated Society of Woodworkers, was described in Plebs as "one of our old stalwarts."[17] The first two delegates from the Council were A. Gwilliam, a member of the National Union of Shop Distributive and Allied Workers Central Branch and H. Goldstone of the Manchester 2nd Branch of the Tailor and Garment Workers' Union.

The Annual Report of the Trades Council for 1922 set out the aims and objectives of the Labour College. It was, they said, "controlled solely by Trade Union and Labour Organisations." It was, "unlike all other adult educational bodies," providing that kind of education "free from and independent of Capitalist bias and control." They also pointed out how essential it was to the interests of the trade union movement that it "should take control of and develop, not only a press of its own, but also an education of its own. The kind of education given by the Labour College makes for Working-Class Emancipation." Knowledge of a practical kind is power and the Labour College sought to "give the worker power by teaching him Industrial History, Economics, Economic Geography, Imperialism and the Science of Understanding."[18]

In 1923, the College held a Garden Party at Dalton Lodge, Victoria Park, on July 23rd. A.A. Purcell, who was Past President and future Secretary of the Trades Council, became Honorary President of the National Council of Labour Colleges from 1924 until he died in 1935. At the garden party he spoke on "War and Education".

The largest class held by the College was in 1924, when the Trades Council sponsored a series

of lectures at Caxton Hall. The tutor was William
Paul, Labour candidate for the Rusholme Division
in the 1923 General Election. Between one hundred
and fifty and two hundred students put in a regular
attendance at this class. [19]

When the Labour College had to vacate the
premises at 32a Dale Street, they moved to Caxton
Hall where the Trades Council held its meetings.
Many trade unionists and delegates to the Trades
Council deepened their understanding of Marxism
and the history of trades unionism by attending
Labour College Classes. Among those who gave
their time to the cause of Independent Working
Class Education were such varied personalities as
William Paul, J. McGee, Harry Ingle, Fred Flood,
Mr. Pendlington, Jack Munro, Jack Halstead, J. T.
Walton Newbold, George Peet, E. Bradshaw, Tom
Bell, Frank Elder, T. McKay and Ellis Redfern.

The Red International of Labour Unions
When Alf Purcell and Robert Williams were
in Russia during May and June, 1920, they discussed
the formation of a new trade union international
organisation with the Russian trade union leaders.
Trades Unionists in all countries were dissatisfied
with the International Federation of Trades Unions
which had collapsed during the war. They were
looking for new policies to meet the challenge of the
times.

The new International was established with the
aim of winning unions from the policy of class
collaboration to that of class struggle with a strategy
adaptable to the different conditions prevailing in
each country. A Provisional Council of Trade and
Industrial Unions, later known as the Red International
of Labour Unions, was set up and a British Bureau

with its National Office at 8, Victoria Buildings, St. Mary's Gate, Manchester, was established. Well known Manchester trades unionists such as Alf Purcell, Ellen Wilkinson, Richard Coppock and George Peet helped in the organisation until it moved to London in August, 1921.

The Trades Council debated the relative value of support for the Red International as against the International Federation in June 1921. The vote was seventy-six to seventy-four in favour of affiliation to the Red International. A report of the debate says that "Reference was made in the discussion to the international co-operation of the capitalist class upon the occasion of any industrial upheaval." The importation of foreign coal into the country was cited as an example. Emphasis was laid on the need for, "international co-operation among the working class on the same lines." The opinion was expressed that "little could be expected from the Amsterdam International in this direction."[20]

Subsequent events proved this remark to have been prophetic. But except for a short period after the second World War, the forces of reaction were able to maintain the divisions that existed in the world trade union movement.

The Manchester Building Guild

At the beginning of 1920, a Building Guild was formed in Manchester under the District Council of the National Federation of Building Trades Operatives. Those unions affiliated to the Federation appointed a Directing Board which was thus responsible to the building workers of the Manchester area. The Board co-opted architects and surveyors and houses of excellent quality were built under trade union conditions.

G. S. Hobson addressed the Trades Council on the "Manchester Building Guild" and explained what its policy was. On May 15th the Council called a Conference on National Guilds and "the question of industrial control was discussed in the light of Guild organisation."[21] Unfortunately, when the slump hit the building industry, the Guild found itself in severe financial difficulties and had to close down.

The Engineers' Lock-out

In 1922, the Engineering employers decided to attack the unions by attempting to impose an agreement which gave management the right to introduce changes in established workshop practices without prior negotiation. They also claimed to be the sole arbiters of when overtime should or should not be worked. At that time, the Amalgamated Engineering Union had 91,773 members unemployed (including a majority of the members of the Manchester District Committee) and obviously they needed to be able to control the overtime situation to obtain as equitable a distribution of the available work as was possible. The employers decided that the opposition they were encountering was unacceptable and accordingly locked out the union members on March 16th.

The men immediately organised. They set up lock-out committees based on workshops and these sent representatives to a District Lock-out Committee. There were few blacklegs because the employed and unemployed worked in almost one hundred per cent unity. As the effects of the lock-out began to show, James Gorman, the A. E. U. Divisional Organiser, said, "This attempt to starve

97

our people into submission is the most brutal, callous, and reprehensible weapon that could be used... I trust that our members will see to it that before long the employers will be paid back in their own coin."[22]

The Trades Council did all in its power to assist. They made a donation of twenty pounds from their limited funds and also "raised a considerable fund through an appeal to the affiliated societies."[23]

In spite of the assistance and goodwill, the members of the A.E.U. were defeated. They were forced to return to work on the employers' terms on 13th June after thirteen grim, but solid, weeks.

Back To The Unions

The depression which followed rapidly on the immediate post-war boom hit the unions hard. By 1921/22 the value of Britain's overseas trade had declined, wages were reduced and it was estimated that wartime wage increases were only worth a quarter of their face value. Unemployment increased to alarming proportions and union membership declined.

The Trade Union Congress decided to launch a Back To The Unions campaign to reverse this trend. Manchester Trades Council took up the challenge vigorously. The view was taken that it had to be more than a back to the unions approach. It must include more positive "propaganda in favour of trade union unity and solidarity."[24] The Council also stressed the need for trade union amalgamations.

After the campaign began on July 2nd, 1923, over two hundred outdoor meetings were held outside factories. On July 8th, the final day, three

demonstrations were held, one at the Salford
Hippodrome, one at Hulme Town Hall and one at
the Whitworth Institute in Openshaw. The
Secretary reported that "much good" had resulted
from the campaign.

Unemployment
        As unemployment became a serious question,
the Council naturally regarded it with considerable
concern. Sunday, January 7th, was designated
'Unemployed Sunday' and the Trades Council held
a demonstration in Stevenson's Square with Charlie
Priestley in the Chair. Alf Purcell, Ellen Wilkinson
and William Mellor were the speakers. Ellen
Wilkinson gave her not inconsiderable talents to the
Council on more than one occasion. She was said to
be "an exceedingly able speaker and she was
particularly good at open air meetings. She had a
powerful and arresting voice and was at her best
when dealing with hecklers and rowdies."[25]   Oliver
Baldwin described her as "small, very small and
red-headed... She is impetuous... She is
intelligent and well-read... She is a good judge of
women, but not so good of men... She is
passionately loyal both to people and principles.
When the two clash, she is miserable... She drives
an Austin Seven, because any bigger car would give
the impression that it was driverless and might
cause trouble with the police."[26]   On the occasion
of 'Unemployed Sunday' she was reported as saying
that "as long as the unemployed kept quiet and
starved, nothing would be done for them." She
referred to the "shameful display of luxury in London"[27]
and urged the workers to ensure that if the contest
for money and food was between toy spaniels and
children, then the children were to get what was going.

99

After she spoke, a resolution was adopted calling upon the Government to "deal with the problem as a National Emergency and provide work or full maintenance."[28]

A month later, on February 6th, meetings were held at Whitworth Hall, Openshaw, and Hulme Town Hall. The speakers were Robert Smillie, M.P., A.B. Swales of the Engineers, and Fred Bramley. In Hulme Town Hall, Robert Smillie challenged the system which created unemployment. He said that he "had been charged with sowing hatred between classes." To that he pleaded guilty. He said that his aim was to "encourage the workers to hate, with all the hatred they can command, the system under which we live; but not individuals." "Capitalism", he said, "has no soul and no humanity."[29] The other two speakers urged the "non-union men to identify themselves with their fellow workers by joining trade unions and expressing dissatisfaction with the present method of dealing with unemployment."[30]

Annual Conferences of Trades Councils

The sharpening struggles of the post-war years brought into focus the acute need for unity and coordinated action on the issues that were confronting many trades councils. The Birmingham Trades Council called a conference on 14th October, 1922 and invited representatives from other Trades Councils. A National Federation of Trades Councils was formed and this called a second conference which was also held in Birmingham on 17th November 1923. It was attended by representatives from seventy-two trades councils including Manchester. There were one hundred and twenty delegates present and they represented seventy five thousand workers.

Harry Pollitt, who had been Secretary of the Openshaw Socialist Society and was well known to Manchester trades unionists, took the Chair. He made an appeal for united action in the face of the attacks on the workers.

A resolution was carried at the conference that called for the trades councils to become, "Active and energetic agitational bodies taking up all those questions and problems affecting the workers, such as unemployment, housing, wage cuts, rents and so on." They also agreed that the trades councils "should admit all bona-fide political, industrial, co-operative and social working class organisations" into their ranks with the aim of catering for, "every phase of working class life."[31] A further resolution from Manchester called for a "closer relationship between local Trades Councils and the General Council of the Trades Union Congress."[32]

The General Council acted on this issue and on 27th February, 1925, convened the first official Conference of Trades Councils under the auspices of the Trades Union Congress.

Manchester Trades Council placed such an importance on the decisions of the Birmingham conference that it "prepared special reports and supplied many thousands of copies to other Trades Councils"[33] as well as to their own members. The two unofficial conferences were lively occasions with wide ranging discussions. It is a pity that the official conferences of later years did not always follow the same path.

In addition to recognising the need for uniting the workers nationally, the Trades Council took the opportunity of the British Trades Union Congress delegation to Russia to make a stand in the interest of international trade union unity. It unanimously commended the T. U. C. delegation for its efforts on behalf of unity and particularly on the results of the joint conference that was held between the British representatives and those from the All-Russian Central Council of the Trades Unions. Manchester called on the General Council to ratify the agreement that had been reached as quickly as possible and to put the provisions in it into operation. This, they considered, "would be a preliminary step to a world wide propaganda campaign aimed to unite all the world's workers in one Trade Union International."[34]

Among those stalwarts who were working on the Trades Council at that time was Charlie Priestley. When he died, in 1925, his funeral procession was said to be the largest that had ever entered Phillips Park Cemetary. He was a delegate to the Council and Vice-President, 1919-1921. William Mellor described him as, "the most lovable and jovial of comrades, unselfish almost beyond belief, a glutton for work, the prince of propagandists."[35] Rhys Davies, M. P., wrote of him, "He was a proletarian to the end; the palms of his big hands were like the well-worn leather of the blacksmith's apron, his fingers had been so stained in the dirt of his job, and his shoulders so broad that you could tell at a glance that he was a workman among workmen."

He was well known as a protagonist of trade unionism. "He had tramped the cobbled streets of his native county preaching the gospel of trade unionism. He spoke at the park gates of every town in the North where there was a recognised Socialist 'pitch' - and often where there was not - and he had slated employers a hundred times over

whilst nursing his trade union foundlings. He
knew Jack London's 'Iron Heel' by heart, he was
Everard in excelsis, and could recite Lowell's
poems for hours on end. He never became a
foreman in the workshop - he was too prone to
watch the interests of 'my class'." His
propaganda efforts were unpaid and willingly
performed for the sake of 'the cause'. "To offer
him money" said Rhys Davies, "would singe his
soul."

"If there was a conference called anywhere
at any time by the Left, he was there in full blast
to uphold the flag; and if the Right wanted any
common task performing he was the man who
usually did it. Both Left and Right were the same
to him; he only knew the working class... He
spurned the blackleg, trounced the weak-kneed,
gave no quarter to those who would not fight for
their rights, and detested compromise. He was,
above all, clean in his morals, honourable in his
actions, and a terrible opponent of strong drink."
He was Chairman of his trade union branch, delegate
to the Trades Council and Labour Party, to the
Cooperative Wholesale Society's Quarterly meetings
and attended nearly all the national conferences of
the democratic movement for about ten years before
he died. In addition, he was a labourer for over
fifty years, performing the "most menial of tasks."
Little wonder that Rhys Davies said, "He was
'Our Charlie' to those who knew him best."[36]

The work of the Trades Council was not
always clear cut and defined. On 10th December,
1925, a Special meeting was held to discuss the
difficulties that arose from the discrepancy between
the decisions of the Scarborough Trades Union
Congress and the Labour Party Conference at

Liverpool. Basically the position resolved itself into the struggle between the Liberal ideas which had dominated the movement up to the last decade of the century and the increasing strength of socialist theory. At Scarborough, left-militant resolutions had been adopted which declared that, "the trade union movement most organise to prepare the trade unions in conjunction with the party of the workers to struggle for the overthrow of capitalism." It also said that "strong, well-organised shop committees" were "indispensable weapons in the struggle to force the capitalists to relinquish their grip on industry." They therefore pledged the movement to "do all in its power to develop and strengthen workshop organisation." [37] Among those who played an important part in the debates were Harry Pollitt, Arthur Cook, Alf Purcell and Sam Elsbury.

At Liverpool the resolutions bore the hall mark of Liberalism. The conference was dominated by Ramsey Macdonald, a gifted and convincing orator, whose true colours were shown in 1931 when he betrayed the Labour Party to take part in a National Government. One of the decisions taken by the conference was to exclude members of the Communist Party from Labour Party membership

When these issues were debated by the Trades Council, a resolution supporting the militant stand taken by the T.U.C. was passed by two votes, sixty-seven to sixty-five against. Obviously, the composition of the Manchester Council reflected the trends in the national movement.

Red Friday and the General Strike

During the summer of 1925, the crisis in the coal industry matured. On 30th June, the coal owners proposed drastic wage reductions. The miners prepared to resist and appealed to the Trades Union Congress for support. It was decided that if the miners were locked out, an embargo on the movement of coal would be imposed. The Government, which was not prepared for such action, granted a subsidy to the coal industry in order to buy time. The Daily Herald published the bold headline, "RED FRIDAY".

The Government then prepared to make full use of its time. The aim was to assist the coal owners to defeat the miners as a preliminary to the imposition of wage cuts on all workers. Thorough preparations were made to weaken the possibility of serious struggle by the workers. Twelve leading members of the Communist Party were tried for sedition and sentenced to six or twelve months imprisonment. On 14th February, 1926, Manchester Trades Council organised a meeting to protest against this persecution.

On the eve of the crisis the National Minority Movement called a Special Congress of Action in London on 20th March, 1926. Among over eight hundred delegates was Jack Munro, the President of the Trades Council. He seconded a resolution on International Trade Union Unity which was moved by George Hardy.

The resolution on "The Capitalist Offensive" urged "each Trades Council to constitute itself a Council of Action by mobilising all the forces of the working class movement in its locality."[38] These were then enumerated and included the trade union branches, the organised unemployed, the Cooperative Guilds and the workers' political organisations. Special attention was to be paid to the organisation of young workers and women.

105

Workshop organisation was to be built up, special conferences held and continuous support given to sections under attack. In another section of the omnibus resolution, the Trades Union Congress was urged to assume the leadership of the struggle which so clearly loomed in the immediate future.

At the end of nine months preparation, the Government felt strong enough to enforce a confrontation. The miners were again threatened with wage cuts and district agreements. Their opposition was expressed in the slogan, "Not a penny off the pay, not a minute on the day". Negotiations failed to reach any satisfactory agreement and the General Council of the Trades Union Congress therefore instructed the printing, transport, heavy industry and building industries to cease working from midnight on Monday, May 3rd. Trades Councils were called on to give every assistance to the strike organisations.

The last full copy of the Manchester Guardian reported the May Day demonstration in Manchester. Appropriately it was 1st May on the Saturday and typically it was raining.

"It was a dreary May Day procession that marched under dripping banners and rain sodden umbrellas from Ardwick Green to Belle Vue on Saturday. Men and women in gleaming mackintoshes and wearing the red and yellow favours of the Labour party; delegates from the trades unions following in dignity behind their banners; Communists with broad ribbons across their shoulders - a splash of scarlet in the drab train; hatless youths carrying sheafs of literature; groups of decorated children a quarter mile long procession... Here and there along the line were tableaux mounted upon carts and lorries; blindfold

May Day—Labour Day
1926.

" CELEBRATION OF THE INTERNATIONAL UNITY
OF THE WORKING-CLASS."

Programme.

The Procession will move off at 3-0 p.m. from
Ardwick Green (North) in the following order :

1. St. Joseph's Pipers.
2. Manchester and Salford Trades and Labour Council.
3. National Union of Vehicle Builders.
4. Metal Trades Unions.
5. Manchester (Borough) Labour Party.
6. Divisional Labour Parties.
7. National Federation of Building Trade Operatives.
8. General Trades Unions.
9. Independent Labour Parties.
10. Beswick Co-operative Society.
11. Communist Party.
12. Manchester and Salford Equitable Co-operative Society.

Sections must not leave the Procession on arriving at
Belle Vue, but will proceed through the gates to the place
appointed for inspection and dispersal. **Section Marshals will
report on Saturday for further instructions to the Chief
Marshal, William Prince Telfer.**

TICKETS OF ADMISSION TO BELLE VUE CAN BE
OBTAINED FROM STEWARDS ON ROUTE.

**Reserved Seats for the Demonstration can
be obtained in the Ballroom at 6d. each.**

Stewards in Charge at Belle Vue—George Smith and H. Williams.

The DEMONSTRATION will be held in the BALLROOM.

CHAIRMAN : **Mr. J. E. SUTTON, M.P.**

SPEAKERS :

Mr. J. COMPTON, M.P.   Mr. S. HIGGENBOTTAM.
Mr. T. BELL.   Mr. T. ANDERSON.   Mr. W. J. MUNRO.

P.T.O.

Justice, her wet robes clinging to her limbs, a
'bloated capitalist' with one hand on a soda syphon
and the other gripping the rope which ended in a
noose around a workman's neck. The banners of
the Trades Unions were varied by those of other
groups, ranking from a sober 'stand by the miners'
to the appeal of the Communists 'don't shoot the
workers'.

Banners, tableaux, raincoats and umbrellas
passed through the double gates into Belle Vue
Gardens. There, packed into the great hall, the
'Labour Thing' suddenly became a tense, unified
personality. The words that galvanised it into
enthusiasm, almost into passion, were those of
Mr. Joe Compton, M.P. 'The trade unions of the
country have decided to call a General Strike'.
For a fraction of a second the audience was hushed
and the wail of an infant could be heard at the back
of the hall. Then a wild burst of cheering broke
out. The Communists waved their red streamers
and hats were thrown into the air. Thereafter
every reference from the platform to 'the coming
fight' and every appeal to 'stand by the miners'
was received with cheering and applause. The
solidarity of the meeting was incontestable.''

The resolution, carried with acclamation,
pledged every person there "especially in this
time of crisis, to support in every way, by every
means in our power, the mineworkers of this
country in their just resistance to the intolerable
demands of the mine owners. He who is not for
the miners is against the working class.''

In the same issue of the Guardian, an
announcement was made that as a precautionary
measure, the Government had moved certain
detachments of troops into South Wales, Lancashire

and Scotland. This was done under the plea that they would be available to assist the Police in the "maintenance of law and order and the protection of life and property."[39]

Manchester did not become a storm centre of the General Strike. There were probably less than a thousand miners at work in the City. The engineering trades were in the second line and were not called out until the last days of the strike. The front line was held by the transport workers.

Following Red Friday, the Trades Council had convened a Council of Action. But in practice this proved too unwieldy since seventy unions sent representatives to it. The Executive of the Council therefore constituted the operative Council of Action.

At midnight on Monday, 3rd May, the all-night trams stopped running. The evening shift of the printworkers caught the last tram home and from then, newspapers appeared irregularly and in attenuated form. The Manchester Guardian was printed by management personnel on one or two sheets and the Manchester Evening Chronicle was duplicated on single sheets.

The transport workers, the shock troops of the strike, were solid from the start. The first issue of the British Worker published by the Trades Union Congress, printed the headline, "Business in a cleft stick - paralysing effect of the strike at Manchester - Men firm as a rock".[40] The article quoted the tramway men in both Manchester and Salford as "standing firm". It also reported that work at the Docks was at a standstill and the Ship Canal was idle.

When a meeting was due to be held near the Town Hall, the Lord Mayor refused permission and the workers "marched away in orderly fashion".[41]

The Labour members of the City Council put
forward a resolution on 4th May condemning the
principal officials at the Town Hall for "acting as
strike breakers in connection with transport in
the City"[42] but it was defeated by the Tories.

On 5th May, the British Worker was able to
report, "All joining in - Manchester's force of
strikers growing hourly". The local position was
fully outlined, "In addition to stoppage of the traffic,
grades work has ceased at the railway workshops in
Manchester and District, including Newton Heath
and Dukinfield. The Amalgamated Engineering
Union reports that its men had struck where members
of other unions had been called out, including railway
shops, newspaper offices and tramway sheds. The
Electrical Trades Union reports that its men are out
with the exception of those employed on building
schemes at hospitals. The tramway stoppage in
Manchester is complete, only the three oldest drivers
in the employ of the Tramways Company having
reported for duty".[43]

The Police took measures to preserve "law and
order" and enlisted a thousand special constables.

On Friday, 7th May, Ellen Wilkinson and J. F.
Horrabin sent a report to the General Council saying,
"Position absolutely solid, but local movement
demands news. We urge publication of local strike
paper which has not been done. N. U. D. A. W.
(National Union of Distributive and Allied Workers)
Head Office has placed private press at the disposal
of the Strike Committee. "[44]

T. McLean, Area Group Secretary of the
Transport and General Workers' Union also sent a
report to the T. U. C. He wrote on behalf of the
North West Region Strike Committee and informed
the T. U. C. of the attempt at intimidation that had

been made by the Salford Tramways Committee. Threatening letters had been sent to the men, but after negotiation, agreement had been reached that the men would receive their due wages, but would hand in their uniforms. In fact, this was not carried out. The men kept the uniforms and the notices were withdrawn.

The Manchester Emergency Committee threatened to move foodstuffs from the depots if the men refused to handle it. The National Union of Railwaymen had issued instructions that no goods of any kind were to be moved. The Lord Mayor appealed for volunteers to drive road vehicles if the need arose. He said that private traders had coped with the position up to that time but that he wanted to be prepared.

By Saturday, May 8th, efforts had been made to launch a Manchester edition of the British Worker. Fenner Brockway was sent from London to be the editor. He and H. Skinner of the Typographical Association were jointly responsible for the production. Skinner, however, was ill and unable to cooperate. The Cooperative Printing Society which was supposed to print the paper was refused permission by the London Executive. The unions concerned in production of the paper met and suggested that the Manchester Cooperative Publishing Society might do the job. But their Manager lived at Southport, fifty miles away. However, transport was laid on and with the Manager's permission duly obtained, the necessary workers were alerted and publication commenced. Socialist members of the National Union of Journalists offered assistance although their union organisation refused. The National Union of Clerks provided typists and telephonists. The National Society of Operative Printers and Assistants accepted responsibility for the accounts and despatch and the Transport Workers organised distribution as fa

as Derby to the South, Holyhead to the West, Hull
to the East and North to Carlisle. Fenner Brockway
commented that as the organisation took shape he
realised the historical significance that for the first
time a British newspaper was being produced under
the direct control of the workers.

While these preparations were taking place,
there was a demonstration on Saturday, 8th May,
when twenty thousand people marched to Platt Fields
to hear Miss Mary Quaile, a member of the General
Council of the Trades Union Congress and Rhys
Davies, M.P.. An eye-witness wrote, "There was...
during this week of the General Strike, a sense of pride
in the disciplined response of organised labour to their
collective decision. Remembering Black Friday of
1921, this pride was mingled with relief for, as they
said, 'this time we have not let the miners down'.
The demonstration in Platt Fields on the Saturday of
Strike Week was imbued with this spirit on the part of
the demonstrators. There was a large orderly crowd
and the presence of many women and children with
sandwiches and bottles of milk made it seem almost
like a picnic. This was the occasion when a football
match was arranged between the strikers and the
City Police which has passed into folklore and which
is regarded with amazement by those who cannot
comprehend the peculiarities of English society.
There was, in my view, no recognition of inconsistency,
for the strikers considered that, as long as they
remained orderly, they were within their legal rights
in withdrawing their labour. As far as the miners were
concerned this was allowed, for the miners had been
locked out for refusing a reduction in rates and few
people would hold that men should be forced by law to
accept lower wages. A sympathetic strike was a
different matter and the government were inclined to

regard such action on so large a scale as a threat to the constitution. Sir John Simon had declared it as his opinion that the strike was illegal.

This attitude was reflected in the speeches of the Labour leaders on the platform. A chill crept over the audience. It seemed there was alarm and despondency in the Negotiating Committee of the Trades Union Council. Faced with the charge of illegality and all but overwhelmed by the forces against them and the forces which they had invoked, the speakers exhorted the strikers to keep quiet, stay at home, offer no provocation and similar clarion calls to victory. Old hands at the strike game said, 'We've bitten off more than they can chew but we'll beat them and the bosses too', for they were conscious that this strike, unlike most, had increased in solidarity as the days passed. Towards the end of the meeting the speakers were encouraging, promising victory if 'all stood together' and the crowd dispersed in good heart. Only here and there, in the long trek on foot from Platt Fields to the industrial districts of the town, small knots of angry people could be heard charging the leaders with a 'sell-out'." [45]

The Government was not idle. The Destroyer Wessex arrived in the Ship Canal and it was correctly interpreted as a sign that it was intended to enforce the unloading of grain. Additional evidence had been received by the North West Strike Committee that two thousand beds, blankets and pillows had been taken to Salford Docks in preparation for strike breakers.

Meanwhile, plans for the Manchester Edition of the British Worker went ahead and the first issue was ready on the afternoon of Monday, May 10th. Fenner Brockway commented on the first fifty thousa copies, "We could have sold three times as many but we only have paper for three hundred thousand. The paper caused a great sensation in the streets. Only tiny sheets have so far been printed in Manchester. Conversations with the trade union officials show that the men are wonderfully solid. The Manchester Typographical Association office is underneath a bridge outside Exchange Station. Two trains passed on Saturday! Realisation of the success of the strike is much completer here than in London. At Westminster one was conscious of the power of the Government. Here the men are absolutely on top."[46]

On Tuesday, the paper was published in a hundred thousand copies. Fenner Brockway said, "We now have paper for eight hundred copies, so I risked an edition of a hundred thousand this morning. Yesterday afternoon's edition was largely confined to Manchester. Webb's transport service has got today's issue to Derby, Liverpool, Preston and Colne. The phone is ringing all day for more. We are rationing supplies to the districts but it is difficult to face the bitter disappointment."[47]

Five hundred volunteers were assembled at Cavendish Road Police Station to await escort to Salford where they were to unload foodstuffs from ships in the docks. J.A. Webb of the Transport and General Workers' Union, reported to the Trades Union Congress that the position on the docks was excellent. The dockers were refusing to react to the provocative behaviour of the Ship Canal Company and the Local Authorities who had attempted to introduce blacklegs. He said, "There is no doubt about the morale of the crowd and I am perfectly satisfied that there will be no resumption of work until such time as the instructions have been received from the T.U.C.."[48]

Blacklegs were not well received in the City. During the day a lorry was found burning in Market Street. It had been overturned by a hostile crowd, set on fire and destroyed. It contained bedding and empty milk churns and was driven by student black-legs.

The Manchester Edition of the British Worker on Wednesday, May 12th, gave no indication of the shock that was to come during the day. Fenner Brockway was among those who could not at first credit news of the termination of the strike. "I was warned from London to be ready for a 'special'", he said, "and just after midday the news came through. At first it was meagre. The T.U.C. stated that a satisfactory basis for negotiations had been reached, the miners had expressed gratitude for the support of the other workers, and the Executives were arranging for their men to return. That was about all. I took the news to the North West Committee. They had had word over the wireless that the strike had been called off, but were incredulous and were proceeding with their business unmoved. I handed the Chairman one of our roneo'd 'specials', and he held up the spokesman of a deputation, seeking permission to call out further men, to read it. Still they were incredulous. Was I sure that I had not been hoaxed?"[49]

A similar reaction was experienced among the rank and file. "In the course of the afternoon while I was on my rounds of the picket-stations, the news came through. The end of the strike had been announced on the radio as an 'unconditional surrender'. The pickets could not at first believe it. They would wait until they heard from their own headquarters before they left their post and I left them, still picketing, to rush home and sit before the wireless."[50]

When more definite news was received it was realised that the terms were only an arrangement with Herbert Samuel and that the miners' lock-out was to continue. The confusion and anger grew. Fenner Brockway regarded the comments that the compositors made as they set the type for Thursday's British Worker as typical of the general reaction.

The news of the ending of the strike was conveyed to the workers. Manchester tramwaymen were ordered to present themselves for work at noon. Out of a force of five thousand, only twenty-nine did so. The others went to Hyde Road Depot, where they gathered in strength and marched into the City. A reporter wrote, "from Hyde Road they marched with their band and carrying banners which declared their determination to support the cause of the miners. A great many of the tramwaymen were wearing war medals and on their march into town they were joined by various contingents of other men on strike until the procession marching four abreast was little short of half a mile."[51]

Fenner Brockway wrote in Thursday's British Worker that there had also been a procession of railwaymen more than twenty five thousand strong through the centre of Manchester and that they were not returning to work. The dockers and Ship Canal workers from Manchester down to Liverpool were also staying out until the threat of victimisation to the railway workers was removed. He said that there was "chaos". Although the headline was "Strike Terminated", there was no general resumption of work. There were two columns headed "Last News Of The Strike" in which it was reported that the printing trades were remaining out because of victimisation at the Daily Mail and Thompsons. The men in the flour milling trades remained out.

Because the Trades Union Congress had been in such haste to end the strike, they had made no provision to prevent employers from victimising workers or breaking trade union agreements. This placed the responsibility for action in such cases on the local Strike Committee. Resistance to victimisation and the imposition of worsened conditions of employment was so strong throughout the country that the Prime Minister, Stanley Baldwin, was forced to issue a statement that he would not countenance any attempt by the employers to force down wages or launch an attack on trade unionism. The last thing the Government wanted was a continuation of the strike outside the control of the Trades Union Congress. The workers were, however returning to work thoroughly disheartened and disillusioned. On Friday, May 14th, the North West District Strike Committee sent a telegram to the Trades Union Congress saying, "This Regional Strike Committee, representative of all the organised workers in the Manchester and North Western Area, urgently directs the attention of the General Council of the T. U. C. to the very unsatisfactory position resulting from the calling off of the General Strike. Employers, with but few exceptions, are declining to reinstate employees, and in those cases where re-instatement is offered, it is only on the basis of lower wages and worse terms of service. This Regional Strike Committee strongly and emphatically protests against this action on the part of the employers as a gross violation of the spirit of the agreement as announced between the Prime Minister and the T. U. C.. They call upon the T. U. C.

immediately to demand a withdrawal of such action and notices, and that the Government insist upon the maintainance of the 'status quo'. "[52]

The Manchester Evening Chronicle, which was printed on the 14th, stated that at a mass meeting of Manchester tramwaymen at midnight it was reported that eleven timekeepers and two ticket collectors who had been suspended were re-instated. The meeting then decided to continue working. That evening, a meeting called by Lansbury's Labour Weekly to call for the release of those arrested and imprisoned during the strike was due to be held in the Free Trade Hall. It had to be postponed because the Authorities withdrew permission to use the Hall.

On Sunday, May 16th, a meeting was held in Platt Fields Park where "a very large section of the audience was critical of members of the General Council." A resolution justifying the termination of the strike was put forward from the platform. The Guardian reporter noted that "although very few hands were held up for the resolution it was declared carried."[53]

The Secretary of the Trades Council in a reasoned statement said, "All that we can profitably do at the moment is to express our admiration for the wonderful response to the call that was issued by the General Council by millions who had nothing themselves to gain but much to lose in the event of failure. By their determination to see that justice was done to the miners not only was the call loyally responded to, but discipline and order were maintained to a degree that evoked the admiration of friend and foe alike."[54]

However, a more realistic and revealing account appeared in a Manchester newspaper.

"The challenge to the law of a cutting off of light and power and a cessation of the post, telephone and telegraphic services would be unmistakeable. However little the Council desired it, revolutionary forces would be let loose. The industrial centres would be cut off from the centre, each strike committee would become in effect a soviet." [55]

After the General Strike the miners continued to offer stubborn resistance to the coal owners until they were finally driven back to work by hunger in November, 1926.

While reactionary union leaders condemned the Strike with the cry, "Never again!", the Tory Government prepared to impose the Trades Disputes Act which became known as 'The Blacklegs Charter'. General Strikes were made illegal as also were sympathetic strikes. Blacklegs expelled from their union could claim damages. Mass picketting was forbidden and ordinary picketting virtually abolished. Civil servants were not allowed to join a union. The right of trades unions to operate a political levy for the Labour Party was abolished except on the part of those who "contracted in" to do so.

William Mellor commented, "... Now that the Trades Dispute Act of 1927 is placed on the Statute Book, closely following that other similar example of relentless Class Legislation - the Miners' Eight Hour Act - it becomes the duty of the Manchester and Salford Trades Council again to fight ceaselessly until both these reactionary Acts are erased from the Statute Book." [56]

Although the Trade Union Congress issued an official Trade Union Defence Campaign Bulletin with the title, 'The British Worker', on 29th April, 1927, the union leaders only organised limited opposition to the Act. Moreover, a movement demoralised by

118

the betrayal of the General Strike was in no shape
to fight. The Manchester and Salford Trades and
Labour Council was compelled to change its Rules
and delete all political objectives. The Council
was no longer able to send its four delegates to
Manchester Labour Party and the name had to be
altered to Manchester and Salford Trades Council.

Demoralisation continued when the Trade
Union Congress embraced the pernicious policy of
Mondism or peace in industry. Prosperity for
Capitalism was the objective. The wages and
working conditions of the workers had to contribute
towards that prosperity. The outcome was that
trade union membership declined. Affiliations to
the Trades Union Congress fell by half a million
between 1926 and 1928.

The polarisation of political attitudes which
followed the ending of the Strike and the introduction
of Mondism led to clashes in the Council. On the
occasion of the tenth anniversary of the Russian
Revolution in 1927, a Committee was formed in
Manchester to make arrangements for delegates to
be elected to a British Workers' Delegation to the
Soviet Union. The Committee decided to ask the
Trades Council to accept responsibility for the
arrangements and this was agreed. A conference
was called at which Will Crick was in the Chair.
A.J. Cook, the miners' leader, who was the
principle speaker, took a critical attitude towards
the policy of the General Council of the T.U.C..
He asserted that "what had happened in Russia ten
years ago was the greatest international economic
event the world had seen."[57]   Seven delegates
were elected to go to Russia. They were, Mrs.
May Dunn, Workers' Esperanto Club, E.Yates,
Lancashire Miners, G.W. Chandler, Railway Clerks

Association, Tom Regan, Amalgamated Engineering Union, Ellis Smith, United Patternmakers Association, Frank Edwards, Hulme Labour Party, and J. Garside, Building Trade Workers. [58]

After the conference, a lively discussion took place at the Trades Council meeting. Complaints were made that some union branches had not received an invitation. The implied criticism was met by Will Crick with the assertion that "everything done by the Council in relation to the conference, of which he himself was the Chairman, had been square and above board." [59] Jack Munro gave him full support. A resolution was carried "that this Trades Council protests against the T. U. C. break up of the Anglo-Soviet Unity Committee as a step away from World Trade Union Unity and an incentive to the Tory Government to declare war on the Soviet Union." [60]

Will Crick was the President of the Trades Council when the conference took place. He was a journalist who had joined his union, the National Union of Journalists, in 1909 in the Ashton-under-Lyne and Glossop branch. For five years he toured the country as a journalist and took an active part in the work of the Socialist Society wherever he was located. In 1914, he joined the staff of the Warrington Guardian and also joined the Altrincham Branch of the Independent Labour Party, of which he became the Treasurer in 1915. In 1916 he was a delegate to Altrincham Trades Council and active in the 'No Conscription Fellowship'. His home was raided and he was convicted and imprisoned in Strangeways Prison. In 1919, when he was released from gaol, he worked as a tram driver in Manchester and became active in the Transport and General Workers' Union. He acted as Election Agent when William Paul contested Rusholme Division in the Parliamentary Election in 1924

When the left of the Labour Party formed itself
into the National Left Wing Movement, Will Crick
became the first President in September, 1926.

References

[1] Souvenir programme of the Hands Off Russia demonstration in the Manchester Free Trade Hall, Sunday, February 2nd, 1919.

[2] Manchester and Salford Trades and Labour Council Annual Report, 1920.

[3] Labour Party Annual Report, 1919, p. 156.

[4] Manchester Guardian, 9th August, 1920.

[5] ibid., 10th August, 1920.

[6] Salford City Labour Party, Minute Book for 1926.

[7] Report of the Special Conference on Labour and the Russia-Polish War, 1920. The Council of Action.

[8] ibid.

[9] Manchester Guardian, 14th August, 1920.

[10] ibid.

[11] ibid.

[12] ibid.

[13] ibid., 23rd August, 1920.

[14] Annual Report Manchester and Salford Trades and Labour Council, 1920.

[15] Manchester and Salford Trades Council Annual Report 1935-36, p. 12.

[16] Plebs Magazine, March 1922.

[17] ibid., March 1923.

[18] Manchester and Salford Trades and Labour Council Annual Report, 1922.

[19] Letter from Fred Flood dated 1st January, 1975.

[20] Manchester Guardian, 16th June, 1921.

[21] Manchester and Salford Trades and Labour Council Annual Report, 1921.

[22] Amalgamated Engineering Union Monthly Report, June 1922.

[23] Manchester and Salford Trades and Labour Council Annual Report, 1922.

[24] ibid.

[25] Stella Davies, The Young Ellen Wilkinson., vol. 107, 1964-65, p. 37. Manchester Literary and Philosophical Society, Memoirs and Proceedings.

[26] Ellen Wilkinson, Peeps at Politicians, Foreword by Oliver Baldwin, 1930.

[27] Manchester Guardian, 8th January, 1923.

[28] ibid.

[29] ibid., 7th February, 1923.

[30] ibid.

[31] Workers' Weekly, 23rd November, 1923.

[32] National Federation of Trades Councils, Preliminary Agenda of Second Annual Conference, Saturday, 17th November, 1923.

[33] Manchester and Salford Trades and Labour Council Annual Report, 1923.

[34] Trade Union Unity, May 1925.

[35] Manchester and Salford Trades and Labour Council Annual Report, 1925.

[36] ibid.

[37] Trade Union Congress Annual Report, 1925, p. 437.

[38] Manchester Guardian, 3rd May, 1926.

[39] ibid.

[40] British Worker London Edition, 5th May, 1926.

[41] ibid.

[42] Manchester Guardian, 6th May, 1926.

[43] British Worker London Edition, 6th May, 1926.

[44] Typescript taken from Trades Union Congress Library, HD5366.

[45] C. Stella Davies, North Country Bred, 1963.

[46] A. Fenner Brockway, A Diary of the Great Strike, Socialist Review, June 1926.

[47] ibid.

[48] Typescript taken from Trades Union Congress Library, HD5366.

[49] A. Fenner Brockway, op. cit.

[50] C. Stella Davies, op. cit., p. 231.

[51] Manchester Guardian, 13th May, 1926.

[52] British Worker Manchester Edition, 14th May, 1926.

[53] Manchester Guardian, 17th May, 1926.

[54] Manchester and Salford Trades and Labour Council Annual Report, 1925.

[55] Manchester Guardian, 17th May, 1926.

[56] Manchester and Salford Trades and Labour Council Annual Report, 1926.

[57] Manchester Guardian, 17th October, 1927.

[58] Soviet Russia To-Day. Report of the British Workers' Delegation, 1927.

[59] Manchester Guardian, 20th October, 1927.

[60] ibid.

GREAT TRADE UNION RALLY!

FREE TRADE HALL,
MANCHESTER,
SUNDAY AFTERNOON, OCT. 25th,
1931, at **2-15** prompt.

ALL CANDIDATES IN THE DISTRICT
have been invited to be present.

WALTER M. CITRINE,
General Secretary, Trades Union Congress.
President, International Federation of Trade Unions.

Rt. Hon. J. R. CLYNES.   Rt. Hon. ARTHUR GREENWOOD.

Mrs. **EDNA PENNY** (National Guild of Co-operators).

This "National Government," is a menace to the Working Class. It is a Wage-Cutting, Starvers, Sweaters, and Interest Mongers' Government.

IT IS DEFINITELY ANTI-TRADE UNION.

IF YOU DO NOT DESTROY IT——IT WILL DESTROY YOU.

TRADE UNIONISTS ALL.—— RALLY
AND
DEMONSTRATE YOUR MIGHT ! !
BRING YOUR FAMILY AND ALL YOUR TRADE UNION FRIENDS

ADMISSION FREE.   Reserved Seat Tickets 6d.
To be obtained from the Secretary, 32 King Street West.
Manchester & Salford Trades Councli.   A. A. PURCELL, Secretary.

Printed & Published by Express Co-op. Printing Co., Ltd. (T.U.), 17 Blackfriars St., Manchester. 64931 (P.T.O

Chapter 8

Unemployment and Anti-Facism, 1930-1939.

The Saving of the Pound (Tune: Wearin' o'the Green).

Oh, Ramsey, dear, and did you hear the news
  that's going round?
The Frenchmen and the Yankees, they are
  flying from the Pound,
So drop the Russian Bogey, let the Clarion
  resound,
We must cut the Workers' wages for the saving
  of the Pound.
The women and children first is the maxim of
  the sea,
And that's the sentiment with which the
  Government agree;
So cut the social services, let misery abound,
The only thing that matters is the saving of
  the Pound.

George Gibson (From a leaflet issued by the
  Trades Council for a meeting in the Free
  Trade Hall, October 25th, 1931).

Towards the end of the twenties, the
economic situation deteriorated and it became
apparent that a severe slump was on the way.
In September, 1929, the Trades Council had to
elect a new Secretary on the retirement of
Councillor W. R. Mellor. Alf Purcell, who had
attained national prominence as a Member of
Parliament and a member of the General Council
of the Trades Union Congress, was in Manchester
and available, having recently lost a Parliamentary

election in Moss Side. He accepted nomination and was elected. He developed the position with vigour and authority from 1929 until his death in 1935.

Alf Purcell was no stranger to the Council. He became a delegate in 1903 and only left in 1923 when he moved to London as a Member of Parliament. He was a member of the Executive Committee from 1910 until 1922 and had been elected President for the years 1905, 1906, 1917-1919, and 1923.

From 1921 to 1927 he was a member of the General Council of the T. U. C. and was President of the 1924 Congress. During his year of Office he led a delegation to Russia and on his return took an active part in the Anglo-Russian Unity Committee. He also edited the journal 'Trade Union Unity'. In 1927, he went to India representing the T. U. C. and worked to expose the terrible conditions under which he found the Indian workers struggling to exist. It was said of him that all his life was spent in the interest of working class unity. He strove to serve this aim at local, at national, and at international level.

When he accepted the Secretaryship of the Trades Council, he immediately invested the Office with enthusiasm and purpose. He wrote, "We have an affiliated membership of more than 80,000. Why, with 80,000 determined class conscious men and women we could not merely transform the whole face of the two cities and secure their industrial and political control by the working class, but we could effect radical changes in the country."[1]

When the Government, threatened by a world economic crisis, joined the employers in attacking the standard of living of the workers, Purcell counter-attacked with an extensive campaign on rents. He visited hundreds of working class homes to ascertain the facts and fought each case against the landlord. His careful preparation and laborious presentation of the case ensured success and it was estimated that he saved tenants in Manchester and Salford about forty thousand pounds. A colleague wrote, "Many a harassed mother is now able to spend more on food, because there is less to pay on rent, and she blesses the day when she went up those long stairs in King Street West and took her place in the waiting queue."[2]

The Economics of a Madhouse

Early in 1931, Purcell analysed the situation in a pamphlet, "The Economics of a Madhouse". This was published by the Trades Council. In it he said, "Today the world is embarrassed by its riches. There are too many goods; too many commodities; too much of raw materials, the markets are glutted. The storehouses, warehouses and granaries are filled to overflowing. The emporiums and shops are crammed." He went on to discuss the productive processes, "New machinery, new labour-saving devices, new methods like standardisation and mass production, new sources of power - like electricity and oil, have all helped towards enabling the workers to produce wealth of all descriptions in enormous quantities. Stocks have been heaped in mountains. Goods have been produced in reckless profusion. Abundance has been followed by superabundance... In each of the leading countries of the world, with the exception of Russia, there are impoverished working classes, constituting the bulk of the population, having on their flank vast armies of unemployed. In Britain there is an army of 2000, 000 unemployed... There are two classes - two nations - the employing class and the working class. The

employing class is a small fraction of people;
the working class consists of the overwhelming
majority of the population."[3]

The People's Congress

It was in this situation that the Council
decided to convene a People's Congress in the
Free Trade Hall on May 9th, 1931. In the call
for election of delegates, Purcell wrote, "The
purpose of the Congress it to marshal all the
forces of the Trade Union and general Labour
Movement, so as to enable them to meet and deal
with the present grave and menacing crisis...
The employing class is unitedly attempting to
impoverish and degrade the working class... We
simply must consolidate all the forces of the
organised working class movement."[4]   The Congress
was certainly a success. Over two thousand delegates
were present from Trade Union, Labour and Cooperative
organisations.   They, and the thousand visitors were
in a militant mood and demanded action. Proposals to
have a break and recital by the Clarion Choir were
vociferously rejected.

The first resolution was moved by John Bromley
of the Associated Society of Locomotive Engineers and
Firemen. It called for, "the right of the unemployed
to full and proper maintenance until work is provided
for them." It also said that, "Unemployment pay shall
be so increased as to guarantee... a proper living."[5]
This resolution was opposed by George Brown of the
Altogether Builders' Labourers. He accused the main
speakers of being supporters of wage cuts and he had
no faith in their intention to carry out the proposals.
He condemned the policy of the Labour Government
and said that it had not carried out its election promises
on unemployment.

Ernest Bevin of the Transport and General Workers' Union moved the resolution on wage reductions and the crisis in industry. He called on "the workers strenuously to resist wage reductions and to seek every opportunity to press for wage increases."[6] E. Frow of the Engineering Union opposed and said that the Engineering Union leaders had accepted the employers demands for drastic cuts in the workers' earnings and a worsening of working conditions in spite of the opposition of the rank and file.

A resolution drawing attention to the danger of war was moved by A. J. Cook of the Miners' Federation of Great Britain. Arthur Cook, a fiery orator, had put up such a fight on behalf of the miners that he had won their complete confidence and enthusiastic support. Conversely, he had incurred much odium from the coal owners and reactionary labour leaders. By the time of the Congress he had lost his verve and was already a sick man. He put the official policy of the Trades Council to "campaign against the war danger, and to prepare to meet a declaration of war with a general strike."[7] Before the year was out, Arthur Cook, who was only forty-six years old, was dead. Bill Hamer of the Engineering Union opposed the resolution on the grounds that reference to a general strike came ill from those who had betrayed the workers in 1926. He called attention to the proposals of the Soviet Union for total disarmament.

The call to "build and strengthen the Labour Movement"[8] was moved by Miss A. Loughlin of the Tailors' and Garment Workers' Union. This resolution, calling for one hundred per cent organisation and "closer unity of all forms of workers' organisation"[9] was supported by George Hicks, M. P., of the Amalgamated Union of Building Trades Workers. The opposition came from another woman, Miss R. Goldman. She rose to her feet to speak and the Chairman, Arthur Moss, J. P., of the Railway Clerks' Association, insisted that she be seated. An immediate protest was registered in such terms that the Chairman was forced to take a vote of the delegates. This went in favour of allowing her to speak. She proceeded to do so in a most effective manner.

The Congress was the prelude to momentous events. The General Election in 1929 had led to James Ramsey MacDonald forming a Labour Government on 4th June. Although the largest Party in the House of Commons, Labour was in a minority in relation to a combined Conservative and Liberal vote. The burning issue was unemployment and the Labour Party had promised in its election campaign to abolish the detested 'test and task' work. Unemployed men were set to work on municipal undertakings for token wages in order to qualify for relief. If they refused, they could be prosecuted for refusal to maintain their family. However, the pledge was not fulfilled and the hated system continued. In July, 1931, an "Anomolies Bill" was rushed through the House of Commons. This deprived many unemployed workers, especially married women, of the right to claim unemployment benefit. A further slashing attack on the working class was the May Economy Report on National Expenditure.

The Trades Council reacted to this situation by urging the Government "to refuse to adopt the report in part or in principle, and to refuse to economise under any circumstances at the expense of the working people." [10] A statement drawn up by

Alf Purcell and endorsed by the Council on August 19th, 1931, commented, "This majority Report makes recommendations declaring for a reduction in Unemployment Pay of 20 per cent." The total reductions were sixty six and a half million pounds and included cuts in education and teachers' salaries, the National Health Insurance and pay for the armed services. As Purcell said, "£95,000,000 of the cut is to be at the expense of the working class."[11]

Faced with these grave problems, the Labour Cabinet split. On Sunday, August 23rd, Ramsey MacDonald, Philip Snowden and J.H. Thomas renaded and together with Tories and Liberals formed a "National Government". This Government speedily pressed home its attacks on the working class.

In Salford, the Finance Committee of the City Council announed the reduction in benefit and said that the means test would be applied in the City. Action against these measures was organised by the National Unemployed Workers' Movement. On 1st October, unemployed workers assembled on a croft near Hyndman Hall in Liverpool Street. Roused by the threat to their already low standard of living, tens of thousands were on the march. "For a quarter of a mile Chapel Street was densely packed with people carrying banners and shouting excitedly."[12] The shouts were slogans expressing the marchers' opposition to the National Government, the means test and the cuts in benefit.

Salford Branch of the National Unemployed Workers' Movement had prepared its case and appointed a deputation to present it to the Lord Mayor. He received the deputation before the demonstration arrived at the Town Hall and he promised to put the case before the Council In spite of this, when the unemployed marchers approached Bexley Square, they were met by an unprovoked attack by the Police who struck out right and left with their batons. This began "the Battle of Bexley Square". The unemployed were in no frame of mind to tolerate such treatment and determined to defend their right of protest against starvation. A fierce fight ensued and at one stage, Police were swept off their feet in front of Salford Post Office and a number of helmets were sent flying.

Inside the Town Hall, Councillor Hardy protested against the Police action and the orders issued by Chief Constable C.V. Godfrey. "The treatment of the unemployed that is going on in the Square outside the Town Hall is un-British", he said, "They are being treated in the most inhuman manner."[13] In spite of his efforts, many of the leaders of the demonstration were arrested and batoned both outside and inside the Town Hall. At the subsequent trials, George Watson, Secretary of the Salford Branch of the N.U.W.M. was sentenced to three months imprisonment and E. Frow to five months.

A week later, the Manchester unemployed were in action. On 7th October, they assembled at Ardwick Green with the intention of sending a deputation to interview the Manchester City Council with the request that they should refuse to operate the cuts in benefit or implement the means test. The N.U.W.M. organisers were told at Ardwick Green that they would not be allowed to march to the Town Hall in Albert Square. One of the leaders, Arthur Jackson, put the proposal for an alternative route to the assembled workers, but it was rejected on the grounds that it would nullify the purpose of the demonstration. The marchers, therefore, moved off down London Road with nine Labour Councillors at their head.

MANCHESTER AND SALFORD TRADES COUNCIL

MANIFESTO,

A CALL TO ACTION.

WORKERS OF MANCHESTER AND SALFORD,

Unless there is immediate action on your part the next few months will witness a very serious lowering of your working and living standards. The unemployed are being subjected to the hideous inquisition of pauperism. Housing and other public works are being closed down and more will be added to the unemployed army.

Now that the so-called "National" Government—really a thinly disguised Tory Government—is in overwhelming power the National Confederation of Employers' Organisations will freely enter upon its ruthless policy of wage-cutting everywhere. The settled object of the employers is the lowering of wages by many shillings per week, so as to "restore our export trade to equilibrium," or, in other words, bring wages down to the lowest foreign levels. Going off the Gold Standard must inevitably lead to an increase in the cost of living. The inquisition of tariffs, which this Government is certain to inaugurate, will further increase the cost of living.

On every hand forces are at work to still further degrade and impoverish the working people. On every hand the drive is to add to your privation and poverty.

FELLOW WORKERS, you simply must do something in the present circumstances. You must bestir yourselves. You must put up a fight in your own defence, and in defence of your own folk, your homes, everything you hold dear.

The Manchester and Salford Trades Council calls you to action. It calls upon you to engage in the greatest agitation, in every conceivable manner, and in all ways open to you. It calls upon you to Agitate, Educate and Organise. It calls upon you to express the utmost indignation and discontent, and with the utmost resistance to :—

1. **THE APPLICATION OF THE MEANS TEST TO THE UNEMPLOYED.**

2. **THE ABANDONMENT OF HOUSING SCHEMES AND ESSENTIAL PUBLIC SERVICES :** frightful fever-stricken, disease-ridden, slum plague spots abound in Manchester and Salford.

3. **ALL WAGE-CUTTING WHETHER BY PUBLIC OR PRIVATE EMPLOYERS.**

There is no reason in a world cursed with plenty, where the markets are glutted, where the storehouses, warehouses and granaries are filled to bursting point, and where labour, plant, machinery and raw materials are available to stupendously add to the plenteous store, for any of this "economic" tomfoolery, or for making the poor poorer still. Wage cuts in the present situation are economic lunacy.

FURTHER, IN VIEW OF THE EXORBITANT RENTS WHICH ARE BEING CHARGED FOR WORKING-CLASS DWELLINGS, and the need that exists for the landlords to practice a little economy in the matter of rents, the **MANCHESTER AND SALFORD TRADES COUNCIL CALLS UPON YOU TO JOIN TOGETHER IN A STRONG DEMAND FOR LOWER RENTS AND BETTER HOUSING.**

Fellow Workers, **NOW IS THE TIME TO MAKE A STAND!** Defend your own interests. In defending your own interests, **YOU ARE DEFENDING THE INTERESTS OF THE NATION !!** The workers, forty millions of the forty-five millions population, make the bulk of the nation.

AROUSE YOUR RELATIVES, FRIENDS, WORKMATES !!!

PROTECT YOUR OWN PEOPLE AND YOUR OWN HOMES !!!!

Let us have the biggest, most widespread, agitation that Manchester and Salford has ever experienced. It is vitally necessary, urgent and imperative.

On behalf of the Manchester and Salford Trades Council,

A. A. PURCELL, *Secretary.*

32 KING STREET WEST, MANCHESTER.
18th November, 1931.

Express Co-op. Printing Co., Ltd. (T.U.), 17 Blackfriars Street, Manchester.   7731

UNEMPLOYED DEMONSTRATION IN MANCHESTER

Yesterday's demonstration of trade unionist unemployed passing down Portland Street, Manchester.

Among the demonstrators were hundreds of women, many carrying children in their arms. Traffic was controlled by Special Constables while the regular force was mobilised to concentrate on the demonstration. When the marchers reached the junction of London Road and Whitworth Street, they found their way barred by a triple row of Police across London Road. The mounted Police were also in evidence. A reporter commented, "It was at once obvious that this move on the part of the Police was likely to arouse the anger of the crowd."[14]

The marchers at the front of the demonstration sat down and those behind for hundreds of yards followed the example. For about fifteen minutes there was an uneasy stalemate. Then police drew their batons and charged. Fire hoses were brought from Whitworth Street Fire Station and turned on the workers. During the fight that followed, many demonstrators were knocked down, batoned and trampled underfoot by repeated vicious and brutal attacks of the police. The demonstration turned left and attempted to reassemble at All Saints. The Vicar of All Saints, the Reverend Etienne Watts, opened his Church to those leaders who had escaped arrest and refused to allow the police inside. Later, Etienne Watts gave his support to many progressive causes. Among those who were arrested and imprisoned were Arthur Jackson, Bill Abbott, Syd Booth, Bill Dutson, Abe Moran and Chris Flanagan.

Our Poverty - Your Responsibility

In April, 1932, the Trades Council organised an impressive demonstration of unemployed workers. The press estimated that between five and six thousand marched with two brass bands to Whitworth

Street West where another ten thousand awaited them. A deputation of R. Moss of the Amalgamated Engineering Union, W.E. Taylor of the Kindred Trades Federation, Griff Jones of the National Federation of Building Trades Operatives and J.W. Kearns of the Electrical Trades Union accompanied Alf Purcell to meet the Lord Mayor. They presented to him a trenchantly worded statement, "Our Poverty Your Responsibility" which had been drafted by Purcel

In the statement, Purcell called attention to the fact that there were "seventy thousand unemployed me. and women in Manchester and Salford, and nearly thre hundred thousand men, women and children suffering the most frightful distress in consequence." Unemployment, he said, was due to the "colossal inefficiency and mismanagement " of the ruling class. He told the Lord Mayor bluntly, "All that woeful mass of human tragedy and despair, privation and want, we represent here today, we bring before you as you are the persons responsible in the public sense. We tell you that hundreds of thousands of the people whose interests you were elected to care for are in desperate straits. We tell you that men, women and children ar going hungry... we want to know what you are going to do about it all. "

Not only did the statement castigate the authorities for their lack of interest in the welfare of their constituents, it also pointed out how the worst evils could be overcome. Purcell called attention to the state of Manchester and Salford, "disordered, congested, dirty, smoky, slummy, old and dilapidated in parts, the roadways mainly uneconomic from the standpoint of modern industry. Turn where you will", he said, "there is waste, monstrous waste, appalling waste." He then told the dignitaries that it was their duty to "modernise these two cities and bring them

Tel. Blackfriars 4157

Established 1866

MANCHESTER & SALFORD TRADES COUNCIL

UNITY DEVELOPS POWER

TRADE UNION

Secretary
A. A. PURCELL

32 King St. West,
MANCHESTER

UNEMPLOYMENT
And the Abolition of the Means Test.

On April 25th, 1932, a great demonstration of Unemployed Trade Unionists was held in Manchester and Salford, organised by the Manchester and Salford Trades Council.

From that demonstration a deputation was sent to the City Councils of both cities.

This deputation made a statement to the Lord Mayor of Manchester and the Mayor of Salford, in which it was urged that a vast scheme of public work should be inaugurated, having for its purpose the rehabilitation and modernisation of the two cities, providing vitally essential work for the unemployed.

The replies, in both cases, to the deputation were unsatisfactory; the general assumption, in regard to the proposed scheme, being that it would be too costly. It was clear to the deputation at that time and since, that the members of both City Councils were labouring under the " Economy " complex. Even in respect of the petty and parsimonious suggestions that were made by our local authorities, the dread of financial expenditure was painfully evident.

Manchester & Salford Trades Council.

Telephone No.: BLAckfriars 4157.

32 KING STREET WEST,
MANCHESTER.

UNEMPLOYMENT AND THE MEANS TEST.

Dear Sir or Madam,

The Manchester and Salford Trades Council is holding a Conference at the HOULDSWORTH HALL, DEANSGATE, MANCHESTER, *on* SATURDAY, JULY 23RD, AT **2-45 p.m.,** *in regard to Unemployment and the demand for the abolition of the Means Test.*

The Conference will be attended by delegates from Trade Union Branches and Committees, Co-operative Societies, Guilds and Committees, and Workmen's Clubs. It will, we are convinced, be thoroughly representative of the organised workers of the two cities and the surrounding districts.

The Manchester and Salford Trades Council extend a cordial invitation to you to attend.

You are, no doubt, acquainted with the policy which the Manchester and Salford Trades Council is urging the Public Authorities to adopt in regard to providing useful work for the unemployed. The statement made to the City Councils on April 25th, 1932, outlined that policy. At this Conference further consideration will be given to the manner in which that policy can be put into operation.

YOU WILL REALISE THE IMPORTANCE OF THIS CONFERENCE IN VIEW OF THE TRULY TRAGIC PLIGHT OF HUNDREDS OF THOUSANDS OF OUR FELLOW CITIZENS, AND WE ARE CONFIDENT THAT YOU WILL MAKE EVERY EFFORT TO ATTEND. SOMETHING MUST BE DONE.

All men and women of goodwill and public spirit simply must bestir themselves in face of the present grave situation.

To Members of Parliament
and all Public Representatives.

Please reply.

Yours sincerely,

A. A. PURCELL,

Secretary.

Express Co-op. Printing Co., Ltd. (T.U.), 17 Blackfriars Street, Manchester.   59632 into full alignment with progress. " In that way, Purcell said, work could be found for many of the unemployed. As for the finance to pay for such schemes he said, "if an appeal was made for subscriptions for a loan to some foreign power, or to finance some ruinous war, the treasure chests would be open wide and the wealth would come tumbling out." In conclusion, he said, "The unemployed will not crawl into obscure corners, into the dark recesses of the City, and slowly starve, and fade away and die". "Do you not see", he asked, "that you must provide employment somehow?"[15]

The Lord Mayor replied in conventional terms and attempted to justify the policy of the City Council.

A conference was next called by the Trades Council to keep up the pressure on the authorities. Six hundred delegates were present on 23rd July at Houldsworth Hall to discuss the Means Test and Unemployment. A resolution was adopted condemning the authorities for "callous indifference to the poverty stricken plight of the unemployed of the two Cities." It demanded, "bold and decisive action to provide work for the workless."[16] Details of the proposed scheme were outlined by the speakers, Charles Dukes, J.H. Hudson, Mrs. Bevan, President of the Women's Cooperative Guilds, and Alf Purcell himself.

Later in 1932 the situation became even more grim. Purcell wrote, "With a stupor bordering on idiocy, the owners and rulers, the capitalist class generally, let the industrial, commercial and financial chaos increase - let the industrial fabric deteriorate and let the country become more like an old scrap heap."[17]

He returned to the same theme in October in his statement, "The Slow Murder of the Unemployed".

137

"Winter is upon us" he pointed out. "Want and hunger are rife in our midst. Hundreds of thousands of men women and children in Manchester and Salford are going short of many things they need: are in desperate want: are going hungry: are suffering innumerable privations. Over three hundred thousand people - at least - are in this dreadful pit of despair in our two cities, consequent on unemployment. Before them lie heartbreaking months of pitiless, starved and shivering misery... The unemployed have the same right as all human beings to life and happiness. They have the right to live. They have the right to work or proper maintainance. " [18]

In February of the following year, 1933, the Council organised a delegation of one hundred and eighty Trade Unionists to attend the London demonstration against the Means Test and Unemployme. A special train took them to London and the Manchester contingent, most of whom were unemployed men and women, took part in the march from the Embankment to Hyde Park.

In the May Day manifesto of the Council, Purcell wrote, the unemployed were "reduced, with cold, official, calculated brutality, to a level of existence far below the poverty line; driven down to and kept forever on the raw edge of starvation." [19]

1934 continued to deal harshly with the unemploye and in January, 1935, the Council held a conference to expose the pernicious character of the Government's Unemployment Insurance Bill which gave the authorities the right to draft unemployed persons into labour camps, often many miles away from their homes.

On March 4th, 1935, Alf Purcell again led a deputation to the Lord Mayor of Manchester and the Mayor of Salford. Recalling his statement of April, 193 he reiterated the grim picture of the effects of unemployment, "More homes have been wrecked. More families have been driven to the depths. More livelihoods have been shattered. More promising lives have been ruined. More men women and children have been compelled to undergo the hunger, want and suffering which unemployment brings in its train." He challenged the Authorities once again, "Will you never really get down to the problem?"[20]

The Struggle Against Fascism

Adolf Hitler took power in Germany in 1933. He represented the most reactionary sections of the capitalist class in that country. Purcell explained the situation to the Trades Council, "Hitler, with his crazed following of militarised middle class youth, combined with the old landlord Junkerdom under Von Papen and Von Hindenberg, and the big capitalists - industrialists under Hugenberg, have, with fire and sword, and bludgeon, midnight massacre, imprisonment and proscription - all the gangster methods of Al Capone allied with the murder methods of Mussolini - established a German Fascist Dictatorship... The rise of this Fascist Dictatorship in Germany inevitably implies a mighty Social Revolutionary struggle, vast, crucial, and decisive in importance for the workers of the world. And it is vitally imperative that our organised Trade Union, Cooperative and Political movement, and the workers of the country generally, should do everything conceivable to aid our German comrades in their trials, difficulties and sufferings."[21]

The Trades Council meeting on March 15th adopted a resolution calling on the Trades Union Congress immediately to "give the utmost consideration to the means and methods whereby the movement in Britain can render aid to the German workers." They pressed home the argument by suggesting that the General Council should, through the National Joint Council of Labour, "start at once a nation-wide campaign to acquaint the workers of Britain with the full meaning of German events, and to organise succour for our German Comrades driven into exile or thrust into prison."[22]

The May Day Manifesto, which Purcell wrote, again stressed the dangers of rising Fascism. "In Germany a Junker-Fascist Dictatorship has risen to power amid blood and fire, midnight assassinations, raids and imprisonments, and the most terrible oppressions of the workers and the destruction of their press and organisations."[23]

On July 8th, 1933, the Trades Council organised a demonstration in the Kings Hall at Belle Vue. They called for international solidarity and a campaign against war and Fascism. The main speaker was Edo Fimmen, described as "one of the ablest, keenest, and bravest leaders of the International Working Class. Fimmen was the Secretary of the International Transport Workers' Federation. He was a Dutch Socialist who, together with Purcell and George Hicks, was a member of the Editorial Board of the periodical 'Trade Union Unity' published during 1925 and 1926. In his speech at Belle Vue, Fimmen said, "The Great War was supposed to have been waged to make the world safe for democracy." But, he said, there was less democracy in the world. Instead there were "more soldiers, and more dangerous armaments than before the war." Fascism was the last weapon of the bourgeoisie against the growing power of the Labour Movement. "With Hitler and Fascism in power" he warned, "a new world war would not be long in coming."[25] The resolution tha

140

Telephone : Blackfriars 4157

Established 1866

MANCHESTER & SALFORD TRADES COUNCIL

UNITY DEVELOPS POWER — TRADE UNION

Secretary
A. A. PURCELL

32 King St. West,
MANCHESTER 3

To the Workers of Manchester and Salford.

RALLY—UNITE YOUR FORCES.

ESTABLISH COMPLETE WORKING-CLASS SOLIDARITY.

JOIN IN THE STRUGGLE FOR EMANCIPATION.

Onward to Socialism !

Manifesto of the Manchester and Salford Trades' Council, May, 1933.

❖❖❖

FELLOW-WORKERS,

ON 7th May, and during the following weeks, the organised Labour movement in Manchester and Salford is holding a series of meetings and demonstrations. And we urgently appeal to you to actively participate in them.

These meetings and demonstrations are being held in association with the Trades Union Congress, the Co-operative Organisations, and Labour Party. The whole organised working-class movement has issued the call for the mobilisation of ALL our forces : to express united opinion and to take united action. The situation is critical and dangerous. Both at home and abroad our class—the working class—is being attacked as never before.

was adopted stressed the over-riding need for international unity, expressed sympathy with workers in Germany, Italy, Hungary, Roumania and Poland who were suffering in internment camps and prisons, and called "upon the workers of Britain and of all other countries to do their utmost to assist the struggles of their fellow workers in the lands degraded and befouled by Fascist Dictatorships." It ended with a call for the "old battle cry of the Workers' International: 'Workers of the world unite. You have nothing to lose but your chains. You have a world to win!' to be "inscribed on their banners and embody the spirit of their thought and action." [26]

The Reichstag Fire Trial

Before the year was out, the world was electrified by a voice from inside Fascist Germany. The courageous Bulgarian Communist Georgi Dimitrov arrested and charged with setting fire to the Reichstag, took advantage of his position in court to expose Fascism. He put his case with such skill that he and his companions were acquitted. This episode increased the intensity with which British workers campaigned for the release of prisoners of Fascism.

In December, 1933, the Trades Council protested "most strongly against the threat of death or imprisonment to the Comrades Torgler, Dimitroff, Taneff and Popoff on the framed-up charge of firing the German Parliament of which charge they have since proved their innocence, and demands their instant release and safe conduct from Germany." [27] The campaign was successful. The Government of the U.S.S.R. requested the German Government to release the prisoners and Dimitrov, together with Taneff and Popoff were flown to Russia. Torgler, who had been a member of the Reichstag, was not released although he also was innocent.

In the Annual Report in 1934, Purcell summarised developments. "At the beginning of the year it seemed as if the rising tide of Fascism would carry everything before it. Even in Britain, where the institutions and practice of Democracy are most deeply rooted, there were evident signs of a movement towards a naked and brutal capitalist dictatorship. But in February there came a check. The workers of Austria rose in revolt, in Vienna especially. With amazing heroism they obtained such weapons as they could, turned their dwellings into fortresses, and fought in defence of their lives and liberties, answering the artillery of their Fascist enemies with fire from their rifles. The heroic workers of Austria were defeated, and the hangman's rope and prison were used to still further the work of repression. Nevertheless, the stand of the Austrian trade unionists and Socialists greatly increased the morale and the will to resistance of the European working class... Huge workers' demonstrations took place in France which delayed the progress of Fascism in that country. In Spain, particularly in the Asturias, the workers engaged in a terrific struggle... It was made plain to the governing classes of the world that never again would the workers of any country submit to Fascism, as in Italy and Germany; submit to the destruction of their Trade Unions, Cooperative and Political Organisations, and their Democratic Rights and Liberties without a war to the death." [28]

On February 25th, 1934, a demonstration was held at the Free Trade Hall to express solidarity with the workers of Austria for their courageous stand against the Fascists. About our own Government's actions, the Council was less sanguine. At the meeting on October 17th, it was agreed that the Conservative Bill "Incitement To Disaffection" expressed Fascist tendencies. It was decided to organise a demonstration to protest against the Bill and against Fascism. Ronald Kidd of the National Council for Civil Liberties, who was the Council's guest speaker, said that the Bill contained "an open attack on civil liberties of thought speech and the press" together with "police interference with our private lives to a degree unknown in the last century." The Bill, he said "was evil and un-British." [29]

The march and demonstration against the Bill took place on 21st October, 1934. It started at All Saints and the two to three thousand marchers proceeded to Platt Fields where they were addressed from three platforms in the park. Among the speakers were, Canon Shimwell, A. J. P. Taylor from Manchester University, Will Nally, George Brown, Reverend Stanley Mossop and Reverend Etienne Watts. The meeting adopted a resolution describing itself as a "gathering in defence of the rights and liberties of the people and in defence of their civil and democratic institutions and organisations." It went on to express the "utmost horror and detestation of Fascism, militarisation of the police and the open drilling and arming of hooligans." [30]

About a year after this demonstration, on Tuesday, December 24th, 1935, Albert Arthur Purcell died at his home in Higher Crumpsall. By his death, the Trades Council lost the member who had probably made the greatest contribution to its activity from its formation in 1866. A close colleague, Jack Munro, wrote of him, "Purcell had a dynamic personality. Wherever he was going, he always travelled full steam ahead. He was happiest when there was work to do. He rushed into it with a vigour that had to be seen to believed. His one and only purpose in life was the betterment of the working class and its elevation to its rightful position in the world... his chief characteristics were his marvellous optimism and his fund of good humour."[31] A general appraisal of Purcell's career summed it up in these terms. "His early days as trade union member, leader and official, days of ceaseless building in a rising movement, eagerly absorbing socialist propoganda, had firmly implanted in his mind the great idea which is the beginning of all working class advance - solidarity, unity, against the exploiters. But he developed and carried forward this trade union idea to heights and distances which few have been able to achieve. His thought was not content with repeating the need for solidarity; he developed it into the slogan "Unity is Power" and lost no opportunity of conveying this conception to the minds of the workers."

The Council elected its Treasurer, Jack Munro, to be the new Secretary. Born in 1874, Munro served his apprenticeship as a sheet metal worker. He became a member of the Openshaw Socialist Society while still a young man and was frequently seen at Margaret Street Socialist Hall. He was active in the movement for Independent Working Class Education and was a member of the Plebs League as well as a class tutor. During the First World War he was a shop steward at Crossley Motors, a member of the Works Committee and a prominent leader of the Manchester Engineering Joint Shop Stewards' Committee. He was first elected to the Trades Council in 1920 and in 1922/23 was Vice-President. He became President in 1924-25 and in 1926 was elected Treasurer. He was also active in his Union, The Sheet Metal Workers and Braziers. He was first elected to the Executive Committee in 1921 and became President during 1930 and 1931. He was

again elected to the Executive in 1932 and 1933.
As a member of the Labour Party, he attended
the National Conference in 1926 and 1927 and was
a delegate to the Trades Union Congress in 1931.
He was also a cooperator, being a member, and
for a time Secretary of the Beswick Society
Education Committee. He was an active member
of the Cooperative Men's Guild. Frank Meade, a
close friend, wrote of him that he was "by necessity
a Sheet Metal Worker, but by choice, Orator, Trade
Union Officer, Labour College Tutor, Cooperator,
Communist and Left Winger generally," and that
he "attracts either bouquets or brick-bats, and in
his career has received more brick-bats than bouquets,
and gloried in the reception of them."[33]With such a
widely varied experience of the Labour Movement he
was able to take on the Secretaryship of the Trades
Council and carry on the work that Purcell had
developed.

Solidarity Actions

Throughout the crowded years of the thirties,
the Trades Council was called upon not only to initiate
activity in response to the needs of the day, but also
to support other organisations in their struggles.
Groups of workers who were not necessarily
represented in the Manchester and Salford area applied
to the Council for moral, financial and often physical
expressions of solidarity.

Although the textile industry had, by the nineteen
thirties, moved out of the centre of Manchester, in
1932, when the employers tried to introduce the 'More
Looms System' into the weaving sheds in Lancashire
the Trades Council accepted responsibility for taking
action. The employers applied the tactic of attempting
to enforce acceptance of more looms to the weaver at

145

one mill at a time. The Weavers' Union then called out the workers at that mill, so the employers retaliated with a drastic wage reduction over the area. A ballot of Union members supported strike action by four to one, but the Union officials refused to act on it. On July 25th, the Burnley Weavers struck and they were followed two days later by all the Lancashire weavers. This action led to a wonderful display of working class unity and a prolonged struggle punctuated by police baton charges, battles between pickets and police and many arrests. In September, the Trades Council convened a special meeting addressed by Andrew Naysmith, General Secretary of the Weavers' Amalgamation. Following this meeting the Council took every possible step to support the weavers in their bitter struggle.

In January, 1933, the Council decided to circularise a resolution protesting against the veteran Tom Mann being sent to prison without a charge being preferred against him. Tom Mann was seventy six at the time and had lived a full life in the service of the labour movement.

Other prisoners who were given the support of the Council were the thirty one trade union and labour leaders in India who were arrested in March 1929. In January, 1933, the Judge passed savage sentences which were condemned by the Trades Council, which called for "complete remission". The crime of the Meerut prisoners had been to organise the downtrodde workers of India to fight against the starvation wages and intolerable conditions under which they lived. Three Englishmen, Philip Pratt, Ben Bradley and Lester Hutchinson were among those sentenced for three to twelve years imprisonment. S.A.Dange, Assistant Secretary of the All-India Trade Union Congress was also in gaol. Lester Hutchinson was th son of Alderman Mary Knight. In 1945, he became Member of Parliament for the Rusholme Division of Manchester.

Manchester's association with Leningrad has a long history. In August, 1933, Alf Purcell paid his third visit to Russia. Reporting to the Trades Council at its meeting on Wednesday, September 20th, he spoke of his first visit in 1920 and recalled seeing the terrible chaos which the war had wrought. Compared with his visit in 1924, he said he found "the powerful Socialist dynamic pulsating through and vitalising everything" in August 1933. He said that life in Leningrad demonstrated that "not merely is Russia practically realising vast plans of economic reconstruction, but is ensuring that every minor detail contributing to the happiness of the people is being given due consideration." On every hand, he said, there was evidence "of the new vigorous youthful Socialist Russia bursting with energy, with ideas, with plans, with really constructive work." [34]

The work of the Council is well illustrated by the wiredrawers strike in 1934. The men at Richard Johnson and Nephew at Forge Lane, Bradford, refused to allow the Bedaux system of 'scientific' speed up to be operated in the factory. Their strike of nine months was bitter and particularly destructive. Richard Johnsons was a neighbourhood firm and the workers lived in a relatively small area around the factory. Since the majority of the people in that district were affected by the strike, their needs were desperate. The Council played its part fully. Meetings were organised to bring together other unions with members in the firm so that solidarity action could be taken. A financial appeal was issued widely and nearly seven hundred pounds was raised locally. At the Trades Union Congress in 1935, Mr. Seed of the Wiredrawers

Society thanked the Manchester and Salford Trades Council, the Trades Councils in the neighbourhood and the General Council for raising nearly two thousand pounds.

Links with India continued to be maintained. In February, 1935, the Council was addressed by Krishna Menon. Speaking on the subject of the India Bill then before Parliament, he said, "the problem of India is going to create trouble for many successive British Governments." He added that he had met with no section in India who were prepared to work the constitution. Moreover, he pointed out, "No constitution will suffice unless it gives the hope of the people taking over power." Answering questions, he said that although ninety-two per cent of the population were illiterate, "if they were fit to pay taxes, they were fit to vote."[35]

Nearer home, the South Wales miners had been involved in stay-down strikes to claim union recognition and prevent the employment of non-union labour. The Trades Council passed an emergency resolution at its October meeting offering support to the strikers.

An instance of Trades Council support for non-unionists who were prepared to make a bid to raise their standard of living was seen in June, 1936, when five hundred workers at Universal Furniture Products in Trafford Park decided that they were entitled to union rates and recognition. A march through the City to the Great Universal Stores in Devonshire Street, Ardwick, was organised and a further hundred and fifty joined the strike. Jack Munro addressed open air meetings supported by officials of seven unions. Financial support was also given and solidarity action organised in the local trade union Branches. A sequel to the story occurred in 1939 when men and women were dismissed at Devonshire Street because they had been organising workers into the National Amalgamated Union of Shop Assistants, Warehousemen and Clerks. Tom Brown, Organising Secretary of the Union and Vice-President of the Council, assisted the strikers and told them that the Trades Council had offered full support as well as assistance by the Council officials.

In July, 1937, the Trades Council passed a resolution protesting against the harsh sentences given to miners at Howarth in Nottinghamshire. They were particularly incensed that a woman, Mrs. Haymer, had been sentenced with the men. These sentences arose out of the introduction, after the General Strike of 1926, of a breakaway, Spencer Union in the Nottingham coalfield. During a strike at Howarth Colliery, the members of the Spencer Union acted as blacklegs and were marched to work under police protection. This naturally gave rise to some sharp exchanges between the scabs and the strikers. Arising out of an incident which was called 'Riotous Assembly' a number of miners were arrested and Mrs. Haymer, who asserted that the charges were widly exaggerated, was also taken for good measure. To add teeth to their protest, the Council organised a demonstration in August which Val Coleman, Secretary of the Nottinghamshire miners, and Tom Nally, Secretary of the Manchester and District Cooperative Party, addressed in Platt Fields. The fund that was raised to help maintain the dependents of those in prison reached over seventy pounds.

Another group of Manchester workers who were prepared to fight for their right to trade union organisation was the Waterproof Garment Workers. After a five week strike by three thousand workers, agreement was reached in which the employers conceded full trade union recognition in their factories. Out of the sixty factories involved, half a dozen large firms refused to concede the right to organise and these strikers remained out for nine months until they were forced to return without success. The Trades Council gave full support throughout the campaign.

Apprentice strikes have a momentum and vigour different from other disputes. This was shown in 1937, when the engineers won a three shillings a week increase and the apprentices were left out. First, the boys on the Clyde walked out. They formulated an 'Apprentice Charter' indicating their demands. They then returned to work. As they went back, the Manchester lads came out and were joined by Clyde who decided to have another go. By September 16th, all the apprentices in Manchester engineering factories were on strike and very soon, there were fifteen thousand involved from the whole Lancashire area. A Central Strike Committee was formed and a representation was made to the Trades Council for help. At its meeting in September it was agreed that a financial appeal should be sent out. Jack Munro gave every assistance to the strike committee and acted as Treasurer for them. The fund brought in more than two hundred and fifty pounds. The strike lasted for a month and ended in an organised return to work. The first breach in the employers resistance to trade union recognition for apprentices had been made.

Spain

The Trades Council had, from the early thirtie been aware of the insidious development of Fascism and many times, especially under the leadership of Alf Purcell, taken appropriate action to make its

attitude known. When it began to be clear that Spain
was a focal point of Fascist attack the Council placed
its views on record. In April, 1931, a resolution
was passed, "This Manchester and Salford Trades
Council, representing 100,000 organised workers,
notes with satisfaction the tremendous advances made
by the change in the system of Government in Spain
and declares its complete unity with the Spanish Trade
Union movement and trusts that the movement will
eventuate in a Workers' Republic."[36] This hopeful
resolution was forwarded to the Spanish Federation
of Trade Unions and duly acknowledged. However,
the optimism was misplaced. The advances made
by the Republicans were overthrown in 1936 when the
Fascists revolted against the constitutionally elected
Government.

The Council reacted immediately and expressed
its sympathy and solidarity with the Spanish workers
in their fight against Fascism. They also called on
their affiliated unions to help by sending financial aid
to the workers' movement in Spain. This was the
first of a creditable series of actions in support of
Spanish Republicans spanning the years of the Spanish
Civil War up to the outbreak of the Second World War
in 1939.

A demonstration was held in Platt Fields to
protest against the Fascist coup. It was addressed
by Ben Tillett, Emmanuel Shinwell, M. P. , and
A. Haycock.

At the March meeting in 1937, a film, "The
Defence of Madrid" was shown to the delegates. The
Annual Report commented "the film created quite an
intense feeling in the meeting depicting, as it did,
the terrible havoc to human lives and property
resulting from the aerial bombardment."[37] In May,
the Council organised a meeting in the Piccadilly

Picture House in aid of the Spanish workers. The proceeds of the collection were sent to the National Council of Labour, Spanish Appeal Fund.

In July, 1937, the Council received the news that George Brown had been killed. Although born in Ireland in 1906, Brown had lived all his life in Harpurhey. He was a tall athletic figure and an all-round sportsman. In the Trades Council he had won respect and attention by the cogent way that he presented his case. In January, 1937, he had volunteered to go to Spain where he became a Political Commisar in the British Battalion of the International Brigade. George Brown was not the only Manchester man to lose his life in Spain. On Sunday, July 25th, a Memorial Meeting was held in the Downing Street Cooperative Hall to pay tribute to the young men who had been killed, Bob Goodman, Arthur Porter, Eddie Swindells, Bob Ward and George Brown. Among the speakers were W.F. Harrison, representing the Trades Council, Charlotte Haldane, Councillor Harry Frankland and Mick Jenkins. Edmund Frow was in the Chair.

Fred Harrison, who was President of the Trades Council from 1935 to 1937, was also District Secretary of the National Society of Metal Mechanics. He had been a delegate to the Trades Council for many years, having first been elected by his Branch in 1898. He had an extensive experience of the work of the Trade Unions and Labour Movement. Speaking of George Brown he said, "I bring to this meeting on behalf of the Manchester and Salford Trades Council a message of sympathy and condolence at the loss of George Brown who was killed in Spain at the recent Madrid offensive. By his death the Manchester working class has lost a leader of great courage and promise who will be hard to replace and who will never be forgotten by those who benefited from his advice during their industrial disputes."[38]

In 1938, the Council noted the "support given by Hitler and Mussolini to General Franco, in the war against the democratic people of Spain, in defiance of the agreement of non-intervention." They commented that this support continued while "Chamberlain with his policy of appeasement looked on with smug complacency."[39]

When a campaign developed in Manchester to send foodships to help the Spanish people who were suffering from the ravages of civil war, the Trades Council gave the Committee its full support. Alderman E.J. Hart, J.P., the Lord Mayor of the City, was President, A.P. Simon, Honorary Treasurer, and Winifred Horrocks, the Secretary. The Trades Council made a donation to the funds and used its influence in the labour movement to mobilise support. In December, 1938, the campaign gained impetus with the return of the men who had fought in the International Brigade. Major Sam Wild, the Commander of the British Battalion, a Manchester man, was with them. Through the combined efforts of the Labour Movement and many other progressive anti-Fascists in the City and surrounding district, over four thousand pounds was raised and the S.S. Stanland left Liverpool on March 3rd, 1939, bound for Valencia, carrying the cargo towards which thousands had contributed.

In 1938, 1st May fell on a Sunday and the May Day marchers went to Platt Fields. Pride of place in the demonstration was given to support for Spain. In the park, three platforms were erected. That manned by the Trades Council had R.A. Bradfield, the President, as Chairman, and Wedgewood Benn, M.P., Councillor James Gorman of the Amalgamated

Engineering Union and Councillor W. H. Oldfield were speakers. The resolution adopted with acclamation said that in the "spirit of international solidarity" they pledged themselves to continue the support given to the Spanish people and "to the refugees from countries under Fascist dictatorship."

The Black Circular

The decision of the General Council of the Trades Union Congress to instruct Trades Councils to expel any delegates who were members of the Communist Party was sent out in a document that became known as the Black Circular.

Discussion on this Circular commenced at the December, 1937 meeting of the Council and continued in January, 1938. The retiring President insisted that any delegate who was a Communist must leave and he named Ted Ainley of the Shop Assistants Union, Sid Jenkins of the Electrical Trades Union and Edmund Frow of the Engineers. These three were therefore compelled to leave. The Council then went on to discuss the Black Circular and the new President Bob Bradfield moved on behalf of the Shop Assistants Union "that this Delegate Meeting instructs the E. C. to place on the agenda of the Annual Conference of Trades Councils a resolution demanding the withdraw of Circular 16, otherwise known as the 'Black Circular.'" [41]

In discussion on this resolution, Jack Flanagan of the Shop Assistants said that Communists were an integral part of the Trade Union movement and no proper decision could keep them out. Fred Beverley of the A. E. U. maintained that each union must be allowed to choose whom they wanted as delegate. Ernie Crowson of the A. E. U. accused the T. U. C. of encroaching on the rights of Trades Councils to

154

independence on such issues while the President said that as an Executive member of his Union he worked with Ted Ainley, but as Chairman of the Council he might have to order him from the room. Only a week later he might be called on to present him with a medal for trade union recruiting and organising. The resolution was carried by 106 votes to 51 against.

During the years 1910 to 1945, the Council met at Caxton Hall. This was the headquarters of the Manchester Branch of the Typographical Association in Chapel Street, Salford, from 1905 to 1972. The Council met in the large hall which could seat the hundreds of delegates who regularly attended the monthly meetings.

References

[1] Manchester and Salford Trades Council Annual Report, 1930-31.

[2] ibid., 1935-36.

[3] A. A. Purcell, The Economics of a Madhouse, 1931.

[4] Printed circular convening the People's Congress, dated 31st March, 1931.

[5] The People's Congress, Printed Resolutions and Declarations, 1931.

[6] ibid.

[7] ibid.

[8] ibid.

[9] ibid.

[10] A. A. Purcell, Majority Report of Committee on National Expenditure, August 1931.

[11] ibid.

[12] Manchester Evening Chronicle, 1st October, 1931.

[13] ibid.

[14] ibid., 7th October, 1931.

[15] A.A. Purcell, Our Poverty, Your Responsibility, April 1932.

[16] Manchester Guardian, 15th July, 1932.

[17] Manchester and Salford Trades Council, Annual Report, 1932-33.

[18] A.A. Purcell, The Slow Murder of the Unemployed, 19th October, 1932.

[19] A.A. Purcell, May Day Manifesto, 1933.

[20] Manchester and Salford Trades Council, Annual Report, 1934-35.

[21] Printed Agenda for meeting March 15th, 1933.

[22] ibid.

[23] A.A. Purcell, May Day Manifesto, 1933.

[24] Printed leaflet, Our International Solidarity Day.

[25] Manchester Guardian, 10th July, 1933.

[26] Souvenir programme, visit of Edo Fimmen.

[27] Manchester and Salford Trades Council, Annual Report, 1933-34.

[28] ibid., 1934-35.

[29] Manchester Guardian, 18th October, 1934.

[30] ibid.

[31] Manchester and Salford Trades Council, Annual Report, 1935-36.

[32] J.A. Mahon, A.A. Purcell, Champion of Working Class Unity, Labour Monthly, February, 1936.

[33] Manchester and Salford Trades Council, Annual Report, 1923.

[34] Manchester Guardian, 21st September, 1933.

[35] ibid., 21st February, 1935.

[36] Manchester and Salford Trades Council Annual Report, 1931-32.

[37] ibid., 1937-38.

[38] Daily Worker, July 27th, 1937.

[39] Manchester and Salford Trades Council, Annual Report, 1938-39.

[40] Manchester Guardian, 2nd May, 1938.

[41] Daily Worker, 21st January, 1938.

Chapter 9

The Second World War, 1939-1945.

> "The heart of the world is filled
>   with shame.
> The world is stained with dishonour
>   and infamy
> Human hands are sowing torture and
>   cruelty
> Despair and distress, discord and
>   misery
> Human hands are dripping with
>   brotherblood."

> The Heart of the World,
>   from Lucifer and other Poems,
>
>   by Salme Dutt.

The Phoney War

Britain declared war on 3rd September, 1939. The Chamberlain Government which had supported Hitler, Mussolini and Franco and opposed the Soviet peace proposals, displayed little enthusiasm for the war. Chamberlain did not want to fight Fascism but aimed to reach agreement with Hitler against the Soviet Union. This was the period of the phoney war.

At the February meeting of the Trades Council, Manchester Equitable Branch of the National Union of Distributive and Allied Workers raised the issue of the attitude of the trade union movement towards the war. They presented a resolution saying, "The National Government, by its policy of supporting the growth of Fascism in Europe, and by condoning and assisting repeated acts of aggression, bears equal responsibility for the present conflict with Nazi Germany. British financial and economic interests are bound up with the continuance of capitalism in Germany. The war will mean that huge industrial resources in Britain will be used for destructive purposes and that working class standards are bound to suffer; as a consequence it will bring in its trail endless suffering to all and hunger and death to many. This meeting therefore declares that complete independence of the Trade Union and Labour Movement from the present most reactionary Government is vital during the war. We urge the Executive to call a conference of all trade unionists in Manchester and Salford to decide upon action to defend our hard-won rights and for the defence of our standard of living."[1]   After a keen discussion the resolution was defeated by three votes, sixty-three to sixty.

When it was reported at the April meeting that the May Day Demonstration had been abandoned, there was strong criticism.

The debate on the character of the war continued and in July, the Executive Committee ruled out of order a resolution condemning "the Men of Munich". Their action was challenged at the full Council meeting and a reference back carried by sixty-six votes to fifty-five. However, on the maintenance of democratic rights, the Council was united. Manchester City Council banned all meetings in public parks. Among many protests was a resolution from the Executive requesting the Labour Group on the City Council "to take immediate steps in order that this ban may be removed." It also condemned the decision as one which would create "a dangerous precedent, deliberately planned by the enemies of freedom, for the suppression of the democratic right of expression of opinion and free speech."[2]   This was carried and later, the City Council withdrew the ban.

The People's Convention
The call for a People's Convention to be held in London on 12th January, 1941, intensified the controversy in the Trade Union Movement on the way the war was being conducted. The call dealt with the bankruptcy of the Government, war profiteering, rising prices, crushing taxation and food restrictions. It condemned "the attacks on civil liberties and the refusal to concede national freedom to the people of India."[3]   It was signed by Andre Van Gysegham, the producer, Michael Redgrave, stage and film star, Lew Stone, the dance band leader, and many shop stewards and active workers in the trade union movement.

At the Trades Council meeting in November, 1940, most of the time was spent in heated debate on the decision of the National Joint Council of Labour proscribing the People's Convention. It was raised again at the December meeting when two representatives of the Trade Union Congress, Mr. A. Roberts, Secretary of the National Union of Card and Blowing Room Operatives, and Mr. E. P. Harris of the Organising Department "warned delegates of the danger of supporting the Convention." Roberts said that if the Council gave support, "action would be taken to remove the Trades Council from the loss of acknowledged Trades Councils." In the "stormy debate" that followed, Nat Woolfson maintained that "the People's Convention offered something the Trade Union Congress ought to have offered long ago."

A resolution from the Manchester Central Branch of the National Union of Clerks which supported the Convention and described it as "in accordance with Trade Union and Socialist principles"[4] was defeated by sixty votes to forty-one. This was not sufficiently decisive to satisfy the Trade Union Congress. At the January meeting, a letter was read from the T.U.C. removing the Council from the list of recognised Trades Councils.

This gave rise to a spirited exchange on the Council. Jack Munro, the Secretary, said that delegates who put forward views other than those they were supposed to represent would have to be excluded. Delegates nominated to sit on the Executive Committee would not be allowed to take their place unless their names were acceptable to the Trade Union Congress and unions which took exception to this ruling would have to secede from the Council. Tom Brown, the President, pointed out, however, that Munro was not expressing the views of the majority of the Executive Committee.

This meeting was followed on 11th February by an Executive Committee meeting at which those delegates who had supported the People's Convention were refused admission. At the next full Council eleven delegates were named as debarred from future meetings. Among them was the President, Tom Brown, Organising Secretary of the National Amalgamated Union of Shop Assistants, Jonah Cunnick, who later became President, and Miss Hilda Brown, Secretary of the Manchester Central Branch of the National Union of Clerks. Miss Brown was an Executive member of the Council.[5] However, within a few months a sharp change took place in the political situation and a new unity was forged.

MANCHESTER & SALFORD TRADES COUNCIL

Secretary :

W. J. MUNRO

Room 104,
Imperial Buildings,
7 Oxford Road,
Manchester I

October 16th, 1941.

Dear Sir and Brother,

WAR PRODUCTION.

Statements have been made at our Council Meetings as to the laxity operating in many of our Factories engaged on Munitions and War Material, and as we are all anxious to supply our Russian Allies with the equipment necessary for carrying on the war against Hitler and his Gangsters, the above Council decided to convene a

SPECIAL PRODUCTION CONFERENCE

to be held at the CAXTON HALL, CHAPEL STREET, SALFORD, on **Saturday, October 25th, 1941,** commencing at **2-45 p.m.**

Chairman : **Councillor R. H. ROWLANDS, C.C., President of the Council.**

Speaker : **Mr. ELLIS SMITH, M.P.**

You are invited to attend. Credential enclosed.

This will be a business conference for the special purpose of obtaining information from the people actually engaged on War Production (Tanks, Guns, Aircraft, etc.) of any weak links in the methods of production in the Factory which could be improved upon, and also for tabulating genuine information and practical suggestions for the increase of production which may be helpful and could be sent along to the Labour Ministry.

As Trade Unionists we appeal to you; if you are really sincere in your desire to aid our Russian Comrades in their heroic resistance to Hitler and his Hordes, you will agree that the supply of more Tanks, Guns, Aeroplanes, etc., will be a more practical method of expressing our solidarity, and will be better appreciated by the U.S.S.R. than all our expressions of good will and fraternal greetings.

ONE TANK, ONE GUN, ONE AEROPLANE **NOW is better than two in 1942.**

Come along with your information written down ready to be handed in at the Conference.

**RUSSIA'S FIGHT IS OUR FIGHT.
RUSSIA'S VICTORY WILL BE OUR VICTORY.**

On behalf of the above Council,
Yours fraternally,
W. J. MUNRO,
Secretary.

NO ADMISSION WITHOUT CREDENTIAL.

The War Against Fascism

On 22nd June, 1941, Hitler attacked the Soviet Union with an army of over five and a half million men. In Britain, the 'Men of Munich' predicted that the Red Army would be defeated within a fortnight. Others, however, struck a different note. On the evening of the attack the Prime Minister, Winston Churchill, broadcast a message to the people in which he said, "the cause of the Russian fighting for his hearth and home is the cause of free men and free people in every quarter of the globe."[6]

The Trades Council had to adapt itself to the new situation. In September, a resolution was adopted welcoming the alliance between the U.S.S.R. and the British Government on the basis of an agreement to pursue the war until a joint peace settlement was reached. Support was also pledged for the declaration of solidarity between Soviet and British people as outlined in a statement issued by the Trade Union Congress. A Manchester Anglo-Soviet Friendship Committee sponsored by the Lord Mayor was promised full support. Jack Munro struck a note of urgency, "Russia needs our aid NOW. One tank, one gun, one aeroplane NOW is worth three or four in 1942."[7]

The drive to raise production of war materials began in earnest. On 11th November, 1941, Lord Beaverbrook, Minister of Aircraft Production, addressed a thousand delegates at a conference in the Albert Hall, Manchester. It was called by the Lancashire Federation of Trades Councils. Beaverbrook thanked the delegates for their "good production in October." "In tanks and big guns of over 20 millimetres it had been four times that of October last year", he said, and then went on to ask

them "to double it in November."[8]   He expressed
every confidence in Russia and in ultimate victory
and forecast that the day of judgement for Fascist
Germany was inevitable. Among those contributing
to the discussion which followed were, Mary Knowles
of the Kendal Trades Council, Miss Florence Mitton
from Metropolitan Vickers' Shop Stewards' Committee
and Edmund Frow from Manchester District
Committee of the Amalgamated Engineering Union.

1942 May Day was celebrated in Platt Fields
with "a large audience in attendance."[9]   A month
later, the Council adopted a resolution supporting the
twenty years' agreement which the British and Soviet
Governments had signed.

By May Day 1943, any differences which had
riven the movement were healed and "all sections of
the Labour Movement" took part in the demonstration.
They marched with banners and bands from St. Ann's
Square to Ardwick Green, where a meeting was held
in the Manchester Hippodrome. The procession
included contingents of Czech, German and Austrian
anti-Fascist refugees. A resolution was adopted
which, "welcomed the Anglo-Soviet Treaty of Twenty
Years which would form the basis of future
international cooperation." It went on to comment
that a stage had been reached where "the world
contains all the elements for conducting life on a
higher plane" and it pledged everyone present to
"re-dedicate" themselves "to renewed effort towards
the cooperative commonwealth."[10]

International events continued to occupy the
centre of the Council's attention. In June, fifty
pounds was donated to the National Council of Labour's
'Help for Russia' Fund which was to pay for a new
hospital in Stalingrad. Towards the end of 1944, the
Council was able to record the "liberation of France,

and the partial liberation of Belgium, Holland and Yugoslavia, on the Western Front and the great victories of the Red Army in driving the Fascist beast from Soviet territory." These victories, they remarked, had "had a heartening effect upon all friends of freedom throughout the world." All was not entirely well, however, for the Council protested vigorously against the Government backing for those in Greece "who so readily cooperated with the enemy during the period of Nazi occupation."[11]

In his Report, the Secretary put on record, "the year 1944 was an eventful year in which our activities reflected a keen interest in the successful prosecution of the war, with close attention being given to the welfare of the workers under war conditions." The Council was looking forward to victory over Fascism and "careful consideration" was being given to "every problem of post-war planning and social advance with a view to offering some amount of hope and encouragement to make the peace when it comes, a real one; based on developing neighbourly relations with all people of good-will, to enable our great Labour Movement to direct its attention to the building of a new and better Britain free from want, unemployment, with its attendant poverty, destitution and all other evils which have been a feature of the exploitation of the people under capitalist rule."[12]

At the April meeting of the Council, the delegates were informed that Jack Munro had resigned from the Secretaryship on the grounds of ill-health. This was accepted with regret and appreciation was expressed for his long and valuable services to the Council.

The opening of the Second Front in Europe on

6th June, 1944, was greeted by the Council with a telegram to General Eisenhower, "Manchester and Salford Trades Council representing 100,000 Trade Unionists, expresses warmest appreciation and sends greetings to Allied Forces under Invasion Command for successful assault upon Fascist European Fortress. It pledges vigorous support to sustain in production and all possible means our Fighting Forces." In the reply, "the great contribution of the workers on the home front" was quoted as being "an inspiration to all ranks of the Allied Expeditionary Forces." It ended, "We wish to thank you for your generous expression of congratulations and pledge of continued maximum support."[13]

In July, 1945, Horace Edward Newbold was elected Secretary of the Trades Council. He was born on 8th April, 1900, in Barrow-in-Furness, into a family with strong working class affiliations. His father was Branch Secretary of the National Amalgamated Union of Labour from 1899. He was later appointed a full time organiser, a position he held until his death in 1928. Horace Newbold served his apprenticeship to engineering at Vickers and joined the Amalgamated Society of Engineers. He became active in the working class movement at an early age and during the post-war years he was Secretary of Barrow Branch of the Independent Labour Party. Later, he joined the Communist Party. In 1923, he was Chairman of the Barrow Branch of the National Unemployed Workers' Committee Movement and attended the third National Conference as their delegate in 1926. He played a prominent part in the proceedings. Because of his activity as a Communist he became black-listed in Barrow and was unable to obtain work, so he moved in 1927 to Cardiff where he worked on the railway at the steel works and at various

other jobs. In 1928, he joined the Transport and General Workers' Union. Like many militant workers, he was frequently dismissed because of his trade union and political activity. After a short period in Swansea he returned to Cardiff, where he drove a petrol lorry for Russian Oil Products. He was moved to Preston, where he lived for five years, maintaining his trade union activity, and then in 1939 he moved to Manchester, where he became Chairman of the Manchester Commercial Services Branch of the Transport and General Workers' Union.

He became noted as a lucid and constructive speaker and debater, and he won wide support in the Trades Council. When Jack Munro resigned, he was the obvious choice for the vacant position as Secretary.

The Council continued to be concerned with the situation in India and was addressed by S.A. Dangi, one of the Meerut prisoners. He had been elected President of the All-India Trade Union Congress. He said, "Combination Laws and repressive measures which were fought in Britain a hundred years ago are now being fought in India." He pointed out that "the textile worker in India with his thirteen shillings a week was a menace to the textile worker in Britain." In India, the lack of rationing and poor transport had contributed towards the dreadful famine which had caused the death of three million people in the Bombay area. Moving the vote of thanks, Horace Newbold said, "In the post-war period, our own social advance would be menaced if the Indian people were compelled to suffer their impoverishment and social degredation." He expressed the opinion that the British trade union movement had a responsibility to "speed the day when the Indian Trade Union Movement could be an integral and influential part of a strong International Trade Union Movement."[14]

Early in 1945, the Council called for the
National Government to withdraw its support from
the Greek Government headed by General Plastirus.
It condemned the attempt to set up a Government
sponsored reactionary trade union movement and
promised support to the Greek trade unionists.

May Day 1945 was celebrated two days before
V. E. Day. Jim Porter, President of the Council,
considered it was the "Greatest Labour demonstration
since May Day 1926." The march was a "colourful
affair over a mile long with banners and flags flying
and brass bands playing." Harold Laski was
reported as saying, "the war was won by the collective
effort of ordinary men and women everywhere and the
time was due and long overdue to put the ordinary man
and woman in power." A significant feature of the
representation on the platform was the presence of
two shop stewards from Metropolitan Vickers. They
were, Hugh Scanlon, Secretary of the Workers' side
of the Works Committee, and Fred Lee, the Works'
Convenor. Both men have since played an important
part in the movement, Scanlon as President of the
Engineers' Union and Fred Lee as a Cabinet Minister.
Their presence emphasised the importance that the
Trades Council placed on the vital role played by
shop stewards in war-time production. A resolution
was carried calling for "swift justice for all
responsible for the monstrous crimes of Fascism."
It also asserted that "Germany's power to make war
should be irreversibly destroyed." [15]

1945
MANCHESTER AND SALFORD COUNCIL OF LABOUR

MAY-DAY

DEMONSTRATION

MAY 6TH

INTERNATIONAL SOCIALISM

PROGRAMME TWOPENCE

Express Co-op. Printing Co. Ltd., 4 Short St. (City Rd.), M/c. 15.   72445.

References

[1] Annual Report, 1940-1941.

[2] ibid.

[3] Printed folder - Call for a People's Convention.

[4] Manchester Guardian, 16th December, 1940.

[5] Letter to authors from Miss Hilda Brown, 30th March, 1975.

[6] W. Churchill, War Speeches, vol. 1, p. 454.

[7] Souvenir programme of the Anglo-Russian Friendship Week, Manchester, November 2-9, 1941.

[8] Manchester Guardian, 11th October, 1941.

[9] Annual Report, 1942-1943.

[10] Manchester Guardian, 3rd May, 1943.

[11] Annual Report, 1944-1945.

[12] ibid.

[13] ibid.

[14] ibid.

[15] Manchester Guardian, 7th May, 1945.

Chapter 10

Labour Seeks its Reward

"All the past we leave behind
We debauch upon a newer mightier world,
                    varied world,
Fresh and strong the world we seize,
            world of labor and the march,
Pioneers !   O Pioneers !

                    Birds of Passage,
                    Walt Whitman.

Since the end of the war in 1945, the Trades
Council has continued to give leadership to the
workers in Manchester. It will be the task of a
future historian to chronicle these events fully
when they can be seen in perspective and their
significance evaluated.

The long tradition of demonstrations has
continued. Each year has seen May Day celebrated
by the Trade Union Movement, marching with
banners flying and bands playing, and the Trades
Council contingent at the head.

A number of outstanding events have taken
place and the Trades Council has played an
important part in them. In 1961, on 31st October,
a deputation of eighty-eight shop stewards and
workers' representatives arrived in Manchester on
their way to lobby Parliament. They were from
Harland and Wolf's Engineering works in Belfast,
and they wanted to draw the attention of the Members
of Parliament to the grave problem of unemployment
in Northern Ireland. On the following day, 1st
November, the Trades Council organised a march
to accompany the delegation through the streets of

Manchester. With bands playing and posters displayed they drew attention to the growing unemployment. As a result, much valuable publicity was given in the press and on radio and television, and later, the Secretary of the Joint Shop Stewards' Committee wrote expressing the appreciation of the Belfast workers for the support of their Manchester brothers.

In 1962, the increase of unemployment in the Manchester area was discussed by the Council. A resolution was passed urging the Lancashire Federation of Trades Councils to organise a mass delegation of Trade Unionists to lobby Parliament to protest against the failure of the Government to arrest the growth of industrial stagnation. The Lancashire Federation agreed to do so and were joined by the Yorkshire, Cumberland and Westmorland as well as the North East and Tees Side Federations. Special trains were chartered and workers travelled to London in their thousands. After a meeting at Friends Meeting House in Euston Road, a demonstration ten thousand strong marched through the streets of London. In the afternoon, the delegates converged on the House of Commons to meet their Members of Parliament. Some did so, but many were still in the queue when the time for the return journey arrived. R. W. Wright of Stockport Trades Council, Eric Heffer of Liverpool, and Horace Newbold from Manchester, with other delegates, met the Chancellor of the Exchequer and other Government representatives. They pressed strongly for more factories to be built in areas of heavy unemployment.

In March, 1963, the Council lost an outstanding worker when Jonah Cunnick was killed in a road accident. He had been a delegate to the Council from

1929 representing his Union, the Shop, Distributive and Allied Workers. He was also Secretary of the Manchester Federation of U.S.D.A.W. Branches from 1940 until 1963, and a member of the Union Executive Committee. He served the Trades Council as President, a position for which he was admirably qualified with an outstanding ability to administer fair and sound judgement, during most of the period from 1946 until 1959. His long period of Office when he was re-elected as President indicated the respect in which he was held by all delegates.

The centenary of the formation of the Trades Union Congress in 1868 was appropriately held in Manchester. A carnival parade was organised by the T.U.C., with the active cooperation of the Trades Council. The march was led by a white cart horse, recalling Low's cartoon representation of the T.U.C.. Behind the horse were forty floats depicting trade unionism and industrial life. Bands and banners and thousands of marchers filled out the colourful procession. A notable feature was the participation of white collar unions. Their floats were particularly effective in the march, which began at Ardwick Green and proceeded to Belle Vue where a huge meeting was held in Kings Hall.

Shortly after the centenary celebrations, Horace Newbold became too ill to continue as Secretary, and Colin Davis took his place in October, 1969. Colin Davis was an engineering craftsman and a member of the Manchester District Committee of the Amalgamated Engineering Union. He had played an active part on the Trades Council as a member of the Executive Committee and as President.

The Conservative Government's Industrial Relations Act met with considerable opposition from the trade union movement and acted as a rallying call for many thousands of workers. A demonstration was held in Manchester on 12th January, 1971, accompanied by a one day strike of engineers, dockers and print workers. There were two thousand on the march, followed by a meeting in the Albert Hall, Peter Street, where Alfred Allan of the Union of Shop, Distributive and Allied Workers and John Forrester of the Technical and Supervisory Staffs Union spoke to a packed audience.

Manchester trade unionists turned out in strength on 21st February when the London demonstration against the Bill was held. It was a dull day as the hundred and forty thousand workers assembled in Hyde Park to march to Trafalgar Square. Many contingents carried banners that had been in storage for years, and as the columns swung out of the Park down Park Lane the colourful scene chased the gloom of winter away. For the younger marchers, it was the first time such a demonstration had been seen in their lifetime; the older men and women recalled the General Strike and the unemployed marches of the thirties. In the Square, Hugh Scanlon was warmly applauded when he appealed to the movement to use its full industrial and political strength to defeat the Bill. This was effected when the Labour Government was elected and the Industrial Relations Act was repealed in July, 1974.

Wednesday, 1st May, 1971, was the Trade Union Congress Day of Protest. The Trades Council organised a march and mass rally to protest against frozen wages, higher rents, soaring prices and growing unemployment. Many factories were closed when the workers assembled at Granby Row to march to the David Lewis Recreation Ground in Salford. There, a large crowd was addressed by Stanley Orme, M.P., R.W.Wright, Executive Member of the Amalgamated Union of Engineering Workers, John Forrester of Technical and Supervisory Staffs and E. Marsden, General Secretary of the Constructional Section of the Engineers' Union.

Eddie Marsden was born in Openshaw. He was one of a large family of eight - five boys and three girls. He went to Ashton Old Road School until he was fourteen. He started work as a draughtsman but was sacked from Crossley Motors in the slump of the early thirties. After a period of unemployment he obtained work in a steel rolling mill, but later moved into construction work as a steel erector. He was an active trade unionist and was elected as a member of the National Executive of the Constructional Engineering Union, a position which he held for sixteen years before being elected full time Organiser for the North West Division. He was also a member of the Manchester District Committee of the Confederation of Shipbuilding and Engineering Unions, and President of the Trades Council. He moved to London when he became General Secretary of his Union.

Manchester has an excellent record of work to further the development of women in the trades union movement and it was in line with its long held policy that Miss Frances Dean was elected as the first woman Secretary in August, 1974. Frances Dean was born in Manchester on 8th February, 1917. Her father was a boilermaker and Secretary of his

Union Branch for more than twenty years. After an elementary education, Miss Dean attended Manchester High School of Commerce and then started working in the Check Office of Manchester and Salford Cooperative Society in Downing Street. Following her father's example, she became an ardent trade unionist from an early age and was Secretary of Manchester Equitable Branch of the Union of Shop, Distributive and Allied Workers. Her activity in the Cooperative movement resulted in her being elected to the Board of Management of Manchester and Salford Cooperative Society in 1962. She first attended the Trades Council as a delegate in 1942, and in 1946 she was elected Vice-President. For many years she was a member of the Executive Committee and a delegate to the Lancashire Federation of Trades Councils. She was President of Manchester Trades Council from 1970 until her election as Secretary in 1974.

1975 was designated by the United Nations as International Women's Year and under Miss Dean's leadership, the Trades Council took the initiative in calling together a Committee to organise suitable events during the year. Frances Dean was the Chairman and Miss Brenda Dean, of the Society of Graphical and Allied Trades, carried the Secretaryship with energy and enthusiasm. The high-light of the year was a grand parade of floats and contingents representing many differing organisations as well as unions which started at Strangeways (outside the gaol) and marched through a crowded City centre to Birch Fields Park. Support during the year's activities indicates that the Council will be involved in organising women workers in the future to a far greater extent than it has done in the immediate past. It is most appropriate that the City

175

which saw two women's Trades Councils emerge in the years prior to the first World War should have set the pace in responding to the United Nations call to ensure that women are given full opportunities to play a part in the life of the community in the future.

The loss of the Trades Council records in the 1940 blitz on Manchester has meant that only the more colourful events in its history have survived in the columns of the newspapers. The daily grind carried on for over a hundred years, striving always to raise standards, to protect workers and give support to those in need, has not been chronicled. But it has been done meticulously, and the response to the Trades Council's calls to action indicate that this is so. Manchester workers have every reason to be proud of the service that their Trades Council has given over the years. There is no doubt that the needs of the future will be met with the same courage, integrity and confidence as was shown by the stalwart trade unionists of the past.

"Hammer or anvil, so runs the rhyme,
  To beat or be beaten upon -
  Whether you stand in the first of the ranks,
  Or be left in the rear alone."

A Song for my Fellows,
Alexander Anderson.

Appendix A

Manchester and Salford Trades Council
Secretaries:

1866-1877	W. H. Wood
1877-1883	Peter Shorrocks
1883-1906	G. D. Kelley
1906-1909	Tom Fox
1909-1929	William Mellor
1929-1935	A. A. Purcell
1935-1944	W. J. Munro
1944-1969	H. E. Newbold
1969-1974	Colin Davis
1974-	Frances Dean

INDEX